G000123989

¡WOW!
Glowing Bride in 30 Days

*Beauty, Health & Staying Stress-free
in the last month before your big day.*

by Laura Pepper

30 Day Books, California, 2011

Praise

"WOW! Glowing Bride in 30 days is a creative fun book to inspire any bride to enhance her beauty for her wedding day and beyond! It has fabulous tips and information from all over the world! Thank you Laura for writing a helpful book for brides and grooms that want to look their best!"

Mary Dann-McNamee, MA, Author of *Wedding Wisdom* & *Owner of Mary Dann Wedding and Party Coordinators* www.marydann.com.

"Laura Pepper has written a fun, practical guide for brides. Follow all of her advice or just a little — either way you'll be ready for your big day!"

Doug Gordon, Author of *The Engaged Groom*

"The perfect guide for the bride who wants to take care of herself as well as the wedding details. A fun read!"

Kim Gruenenfelder, Author of *There's Cake in My Future* & *A Total Waste of Make Up*

"A great resource for brides who want their wedding experience to be both manageable and meaningful. Laura has done the research and takes the stress out of the wedding planning period by offering practical advice from someone who has been there. Her tips extend beyond just the "doing" of wedding planning to provide frazzled fiancés comforting advice on "being" as well."

Christine Hassler, Author of *20 Something, 20 Everything & 20 Something Manifesto, Life Coach, Speaker* www.christinehassler.com

For information, contact 30 Day Books, 661 South Edenfield Avenue, California 91723.

www.30daybooks.com

The book includes personal experiences as well as information from several sources. It is published for general reference and is not intended to be a substitute for independent verification by readers when necessary or appropriate. The book is sold with the understanding that neither the author nor the publisher is engaged in rendering any psychological or medical advice. The publisher and author disclaim any personal liability, directly or indirectly, for advice or information presented within. The manuscript has been prepared with utmost care and diligence and every effort has been made to ensure the accuracy and completeness of the information contained. However we assume no responsibility for errors, inaccuracies or inconsistencies.

EDITED BY ALLISON ITTERLY

Author Image by Luis Hsu

1st Edition March 2011

Includes index.

ISBN: 978-0-9831701-0-5

1. Bridal 2. Beauty 3. Health 4. Self-Improvement.

For my Mum and Little Sister.

The best friends a bride could ever want.

Contents Page

Part I—Beauty

Some Pearls of Wisdom, Food and Drinks that Stain and What You Can Do About It, Teeth Whitening, Top 3 At-Home Whitening Treatments.

Teeth Regime for 30 Days.

The Japanese Godmother of Skincare, Understanding Your Skin Type, Exfoliation, Oily Skin, Dry Skin, Normal Skin, Combination Skin, Sensitive Skin, Blimmin' Blackheads, Wicked Whiteheads, Red Acne and Pimples, Keeping Your Skin Clear, To Facial or Not?, At-Home Facial, Minimizing Pores, Glowing Advice from Greece, Top 3 Treatments for Bacne, Keeping Skin Young for Life, Humidifiers & Sun Protection, Eye Cream.

Clear Skin 30 Day Regime.

Faux Eyelashes—Top 3 Options on the Market, How to Apply Faux Eyelashes, Eyelash-boosting Products, Mascara, Eye Puffiness/Bags, Top 3 ways to Avoid Eye Puffiness, Eyebrows and Face Shape, How to Shape Your Brows.. Successfully.

30 Day Regime.

Shaving, Waxing, Sugar Waxing/Sugaring, Depilatory Cream, Laser Hair Removal, Epilation, Facial Hair, The Bikini Wax, Deciphering the Bikini Wax Menu.

Hair Removal 30 Day Regime.

Beauty Products to Avoid, For You Au Naturale Ladies, Cellulite, Stretch Marks, Advice from Africa.

Part II - Health

Why Water is So Great for You, 7 Reasons Why You Should be Drinking More Water, How Much Water?, Chinese Medicine and Water Temperature.

Getting the Most out of Your Calories, Super foods— The Top 12, The Organic Debate, Vitamins/ Minerals Often Lacking in Young Women, Recommended Multi-Vitamin Brands, Stomach Trouble, Avoiding Bloating, Constipation, A 30 Day Meal Plan to Increase the Amount of Fiber in Your Diet, Eating Out and Portion Size, 8 Simple Rules to Healthy Eating Out, Healthy Dining Finder, Snacking - Healthy Snack Ideas, Drinks - Alcoholic, Non-Alcoholic, Smoothies, Breakfast.

Nutrition 30 Day Regime.

One Newly Wed's Experience, More than Stress—the Pre-Wedding Blues, Why Marriage Rocks!

Wow! Glowing Bride in 30 Days.

Beauty. Health. Staying Stress-Free!

Introduction

What's It All About?

This book is written for you - the busy bride-to-be who wants to look and feel her best on her big day, but has a real life too! Sometimes everything else takes priority before yourself, and the dream to look stunning and feel fantastic on your wedding day feels impossible when there are not enough hours in the day and you are just too exhausted with all the wedding planning. Stress, sleep-deprivation and emotions can also take a toll on your health and well-being.

After preparing for my own wedding in 2010, I had the idea to write this guide - to put together all of the information you the bride to be would ever want to know in order to look and feel wonderful. To confirm that others felt the way I did, I contacted all of the newly weds I knew, plus an army of others that I was referred to along the way. I sent out questionnaires and asked them about their experiences before the wedding - what areas of their health and beauty they were most concerned with, the kinds of emotions they had dealt with pre-wedding, how much time they had to focus on themselves, the mishaps that occurred on their wedding day.

I also contacted a ton of brides to be, and asked them about their hopes and visions for the wedding day - what they were hoping to work on, what their fears were, what measures they were taking to not get sick, and so on.

From these surveys I had the evidence that I needed - busy brides still want to look great, but there is simply not as much time and energy as they had hoped for, because wedding planning is so draining and time-consuming. I also learned that there are a whole host of emotional issues connected with getting married that are overlooked in romantic movies and the media.

I knew then, as I know now, that there was a need for a no-nonsense, easy to follow collection of advice for brides like you and I - those who want to look and feel fantastic for the wedding, but not let it take over their life because, well, life still goes on. Set aside 30 days to focus on YOU pre-wedding, and you will 'glow' from the inside out!

In this guide you'll find advice on all of the topics and queries that were brought up by the brides to be and newly weds in that first questionnaire I sent out. Since then I have personally met with newly weds to collect their top tips and experiences, and when we couldn't offer the advice needed, I met with the experts - a bridal makeup artist, a nutritionist, a psychotherapist, a medical doctor, a hair stylist, a skin specialist and so on, to get the answers.

Why 30 Days?

Let's face it, us gals are pretty busy even when we don't have a wedding to plan. And we're supposed to plan this huge party AND be the belle of the ball? The newly-weds I spoke to told me time and time again that with only 2-6 weeks before the wedding, when most of the preparations were under control, did they have time to focus on themselves. But one thing was true of all the brides interviewed—looking and feeling their best on their wedding day was really important to them!

30 days is a do-able amount of time to focus on you. This guide takes all of the hard work out of researching what you may want to know before your wedding, from the best way to keep your skin clear, to toning your arms and upper back, being on your period, what to eat to avoid stomach problems, how to get a great night's sleep, and even dealing with difficult family members and friends. You'll save a lot of time trying to gather this information from other sources—it's all right here!

How Should I Use this Book?

Feel free to flip from one section to another—you won't get lost in the story. As a busy bride-to-be, I don't expect you to have time to sit down and read it from cover to cover. Each section stands alone as good-girlfriend advice, and you can choose the sections that are important to you. I have included links to online resources throughout the book so that you can expand your knowledge, confer with other brides, or hear more experiences and stories. As a writer and author, I believe that the printed book should not fight with the online world, but embrace it. There are a lot of useful information, tools, and resources online, and I have tried to point you in the direction of the stuff that I believe to be truly helpful and valuable (and avoid the crap along the way). Find these website URL's peppered throughout this guide.

And the Calendar?

The calendar at the beginning of this book is for you to write in any appointments or to-do's over the next 30 days. You can start filling it in once you have read the sections on the areas you are interested in improving. Notes accompany the calendar to give you some pointers.

Use the table of contents and index to dig into the relevant sections when you are in need of some information.

Most of the advice can be implemented in 30 days, but some other tips might take longer to see results. Since getting married isn't about the wedding day at all but the many years that follow it, you can use this guidance well into your marriage!

Anything Else?

You are about to enter such a wonderful phase of your life. I hope that the wedding and the months and years that follow are everything you hope for and much, much more. Marriage has been getting a bad rap recently, what with all of the celebrity divorces and scandals in the media. What the media doesn't report on are the positives - marriage is an amazing experience, though of course like anything worth doing it takes some work. I love marriage and I'm pretty sure you will too. Congratulations!

A note on the products mentioned in the guide: You will find product recommendations dotted throughout the guide. These are not advertisements and are in no way sponsored by the companies manufacturing them! Rather they are what I, and ladies I interviewed, found to be the best on the market as well as expert recommendations. Prices are correct at the time of going to press, but may vary from store to store.

About the Author

Laura Pepper describes herself as a "travel freak, researcher, writer, blogger, and student of life." Born and raised in the UK, she graduated with a BS in Psychology and headed to Japan to teach English in high schools. It was during her time in Asia that her love began as she traveled to 15 countries in a four-year period.

"I met so many beautiful women along the way—both inside and outside, married and single— and I always asked what their secrets were. I grilled this one woman in China (with the help of a translator!) to find out how on earth she made it to 40, with a child, and not a single wrinkle on her face! Women all over the world are interested in and talk about the same things, and we really can all learn a lot from each other - mentally, spiritually and physically."

Find these cultural "tidbits"- knowledge garnered from a variety of backgrounds and cultures, throughout the guide.

Laura met the love of her life in Tokyo where she had moved to pursue both her personal and professional writing career. They were married in the summer of 2010.

They now live in California with their troublesome puppy Sunny.

Calendar

After reading the sections you are interested in, and using the notes on the next page as pointers, you can use this calendar to make notes about the next 30 days ahead.

30 Day Calendar

1	2	3	4	5	6	7
		Big Day!				

30 Day Regime

Some examples to help you fill out your calendar!

Facial *Head Massage* **Increase Water Intake** *Buy Vitamins*

Arm-toning Exercises *Try Superfoods* **Start Sleep Routine**

Dentist Appointment **Get Hair Cut/ Colored** *Finish Trying New Products*

Begin Exfoliation *Workout* **Relax With Friend** *Bond With Mom*

Eyebrow Wax *Begin Teeth Whitening Program* **Practice False Eyelashes**

Manicure **Pedicure** *Hair Removal* **Avoid Salt & Caffeine**

Prepare Emergency Kit **Spray Tan** *Go Product Shopping* **Makeup Trial**

Part I

Beauty

"WE ARE ALL OF US STARS, AND WE DESERVE TO TWINKLE."

MARILYN MONROE

*L*ike ladies around the globe, you wish to look your best on your wedding day, right? Whether you are a cosmetic junkie or never give a second thought to the way you look, it is the one day of your life when all eyes are on you (and cameras too).

Beauty is fun, but it is also hard work! The good news is that you don't need to do it all. Don't let the media and all its airbrushing scare you - the real value in cosmetics, products, and making ourselves "beautiful" is the increased self esteem and self-love we gain from it. So work on improving the areas you are not confident about and let the rest be au naturale. As Judy Garland preached, we shouldn't strive to be anything but a first-rate version of ourselves, not a second-rate version of someone else!

So, use this section to choose the areas that you would like to improve on, whether you want your teeth to be whiter, your skin to be clearer, or to learn how to do your own makeup for your big day. Skim past those areas that you don't need help with (or you already feel confident about), and you have your plan of action for the 30 days ahead!

Teeth

> "I DON'T BRUSH MY TEETH. I RINSE MY MOUTH OUT WITH SODA AFTER I EAT. I WAS PRETTY SURE DR. PEPPER WAS A DENTIST."
>
> —BRITTANY, GLEE

Some Pearls of Wisdom

Growing up in England, there was very little emphasis placed on having white teeth. To the average Brit, white teeth are reserved for Hollywood stars. Of course this might be an excuse to continue the tea-drinking habit that still remains a British obsession today!

Having lived in Japan for several years during my early 20's, the same can be said for white teeth's place in the Japanese society. TV personalities, actors and so-called "idols" often have, what would look like to the average American, discolored and uneven teeth. Teenagers rarely wear braces, and tooth-whitening products do not dominate the beauty industry as they do in the States. Uneven teeth are considered "cute" to your average Japanese person.

One theory as to why teeth don't gain such attention in these countries is that in both the UK and Japan, dental care is not only limited to those who can afford dental insurance, but it is free for under 16's in the UK and very affordable for Japanese students, company employees and their families. So white, perfect teeth never developed the kind of status symbol it holds here in the US since it isn't necessarily an indication of wealth or class.

Regardless of whether white teeth are a status symbol or not, a pair of nice, clean white teeth can do wonders to make you look healthier, sexier, and younger. Not to mention the health and financial benefits of maintaining a fresh, clean, immaculate set!

The First Step to Pearly Whites - Avoiding Products that Stain

Ok, here is the bad news. In addition to red wine, coffee and tea, several types of foods can stained of your teeth. Imagine the stains on your tea or coffee mugs, but on your teeth—not a pleasant thought! The good news is that unless you really want a pair of Tom Cruise whiter-than-whites, you don't have to forego those wonderful little luxuries in order to maintain a nice set of gnashers.

Food and Drinks that Stain & What You Can Do About It

- Coffee—One of the worst culprits. To avoid the harsh staining effects, try drinking iced coffee with a straw. If you prefer the hot stuff, dilute it with milk to dilute the color and lessen the harsh effects. You can also reduce the effects of coffee by sipping water within 30 seconds of each sip.

- Tea—black tea is the main offender, so switch up black tea with white or green tea. Green tea is especially great for your teeth because it acts in the same way as an antibacterial mouthwash. White tea, since it is colorless, simply won't stain, period.

- Fruit juice/Soda (especially cola)—Always use a straw.

- Cigarettes—There's no option other than quitting, really.

- After a large meal, brush your teeth. If this is not possible, use chewing gum or a mouthwash. Especially after eating the following foods:

* Berries—all kinds due to their strong coloring;

* Soy sauce;

* Curry.

One Exception!!

After drinking red wine, do not brush your teeth right away! Red wine is very acidic, so brushing after drinking it will wear away the enamel on your teeth. Instead, rinse your mouth with a mouthwash or chew gum post wine-drinking.

Try to brush your teeth after all your meals, and use gum or a mouthwash after all drinks and snacks. Consider using tooth floss too. As a bonus, researchers at Harvard Medical School found that flossing can add one year to your life! There's a pretty clear link between gum disease and heart disease—flossing is your best bet at preventing both.

Teeth Whitening

No matter how careful you are at avoiding staining food and drinks, teeth naturally yellow over time, and for your big day you might want to turn them a few shades lighter. If you decide to embark on a whitening program, teeth should be super clean (so that the peroxide is bleaching the enamel and not the plaque!) It is wise to book a dentist appointment for a thorough professional cleaning before beginning a whitening program.

A standard cleaning at the dentist will require one office visit, takes between 30-60 minutes, and will remove any signs of plaque and tartar, which will prevent gum disease in the future, the leading cause of dental problems.

Tip: *Before embarking on a tooth-whitening regime, it is important to assess the kind of staining you have on your teeth. If you see a yellow tinge, this means that the peroxide found in at-home treatments will be effective. If, however, the staining is a kind of grayish color, the staining is most likely from within and peroxide will not work. This grayish staining often affects those with fair skin, as the enamel of their teeth is thinner. The only way to fix this staining is through bonding or veneers, which will require a trip to the dentist and some added expense.*

The great news is that teeth-whitening technology has advanced so much in recent years that it is no longer necessary to pay hundreds of dollars at the dentist, and, whilst the at-home treatments may take a little longer to see results, they are certainly effective.

Consumer Reports on At-home Whitening

Consumer Reports tested the whitening results of eight at-home whitening products, and their clear winner was the Crest Whitestrips Supreme. This product was also the most expensive kit Consumer Reports tested at $47. These kits are available only at limited online stores— Amazon. com, dentist.net, smilox.com. (See the box below.)

A similar, and more accessible option, are the Crest Whitestrips Premium, which are available at most local drugstores.

Takes: 2 x 30 minutes for 2 weeks, **Cost**: $34.99 for 28 strips.

Top 3 Whitening Treatments

1. **Crest Whitestrips Supreme Professional Strength Full Kit** *(84 strips)*

Takes: *2 x 30 minutes a day for 2 weeks.* **Result***: 2 shades lighter.* **Cost:** *$47.*

(This is professional-strength hydrogen peroxide. If your teeth are sensitive, high levels of peroxide may cause sensitivity. Stop using if this happens!)

2. **Aquafresh White Tray**

Takes: *45 minutes a day for 1 week.* **Result:** *2 shades lighter.* **Cost***: $35*

3. Colgate Simply White Advanced Whitening Gel

Takes: *2 minutes a day, 2 x a day for 2 weeks.* **Result:** *1 shade lighter.* **Cost:** *$6-10.*

Please note: If you have sensitive teeth, it is more than likely that you will experience tenderness when whitening your teeth. A simple way to avoid this sensitivity is to do your treatment every other day—this way you can still achieve the smile you want in 30 days.

If you do prefer an in-office laser treatment, Zoom! is a quick and easy option, which has improved in recent years to reduce the sensitivity felt by users. The whole process takes less than one hour, and you can expect results of 3 shades lighter or so. Prices vary hugely from location to location, with more competitive areas offering the treatment for $99, and other offices charging as much as $500. Visit **www.zoomnow.com** to find an appointment near you (just enter your zip code) and don't forget to shop around for the best price!

Regime for The 30 Days (Checklist)

Book a dentist appointment *for the second or third week of your 30 day regime for a thorough cleaning. The cost of a standard tooth exam and cleaning ranges from $50-$130. Dental insurance should cover some, or all of this cost. If you live near a dental school, you can often see a trainee dental student for a clean at a snip of the price. Just be sure to ask about his/her experience! To find your nearest dental school, check* **www.dentalsite.com.**

In-office whitening—*Visit* **www.zoomnow.com** *to search for in-house whitening if you have chosen this option.*

At- home whitening—*see the top 3 treatments to find the most convenient option for you. Begin whitening in week 2 or 3, soon after your dentist appointment.*

Follow up your whitening regime with **a whitening toothpaste and mouthwash**. *(Avoid dark colored mouthwashes as they may actually contribute to staining.)*

Enhance your routine with a whitening **floss, gum, and carry your toothbrush in your purse this month.**

Skin

"LOVE IS A GREAT BEAUTIFIER."

LOUISA MAY ALCOTT

Worldly Advice

The Japanese Godmother of skincare (and author of The Japanese Skincare Revolution - How to Have the Most Beautiful Skin of Your Life At Any Age), Chizu Saeki touts what I'd already discovered to work on my hubby who, bless, has suffered from skin trouble (oily, acne-prone) since his childhood. In an attempt to remove the excess oil from his face, he religiously washed it twice a day with products designed for those with troubled skin. Having been blessed with relatively clear skin myself, and an incredibly lazy skin care routine of washing only with water throughout my teenage years and early twenties, this seemed counterproductive to me.

I encouraged my husband to stop using the products and wash his face in the shower each morning with a regular facial wash and once at night with water. The results were very noticeable and almost immediate, and it seemed that what I'd discovered through my own laziness was true—all the washing and contact with chemical skin products was exasperating the oil production on his face, and, in turn, causing the acne. It was a vicious circle. A few months into this regime his skin improved dramatically.

In a similar vein, Chizu Saeki describes the common problem of over-feeding the skin. She describes how some of us put too many products on our skin, thus impairing the skin's natural ability to clean and function normally. This results in a vicious cycle. What Saeki recommends is a skin "detox" or fast once a week in order for our skin to achieve its own healing power. By doing nothing to our skin for one day a week—no makeup, no cream, no skincare products—the skin can rest, rejuvenate, and find it's natural rhythm.

Gosh, the skin is the biggest organ we have and most likely the biggest concern on your day. 20 square feet of exposed epidermis! (Well, not all of it is going to be on show, one hopes.)

Beautiful skin is a sign that the body is functioning correctly. This means that as waste is being eliminated efficiently, food is being digested effectively, and nutrients are being carried around in the way that they are supposed to. Skin also reveals so much about our lifestyle—are you eating right, getting enough sleep, are you stressed out? It is no wonder that in evolutionary terms clear, healthy-looking skin is deemed such an important part of attraction to your perspective mate. It is the window into your internal body telling him that you are ready to make fine, fit babies. Or not!

If you find yourself with pimples, dry skin, puffiness, or excessive oil on your skin, this is your body telling you that you might want to make some changes, either by changing something from the inside, or eliminating something from your external environment that is not jibing with you.

From watching TV commercials, you might fall into the trap so many of us do and believe that slathering your face with miracle products will solve your skins problems. Unfortunately, this is a short-term fix and it won't get rid of the problem for good. Products might improve the skin's appearance

for a few days, but a longer-term and more effective approach is to make changes from the inside—that is your diet and lifestyle. (Sorry girl, no pain, no gain!)

Understanding Your Skin Type

We can roughly divide your skin into one of four types. (Roughly is the key point here—don't get fixated on one type; it can change with the seasons, age and with pregnancy). Determining which category you fall in to is the first step in deciding what you can do to develop your *dream dermis*.

Try This!

To find out which category you fall into, clean your face with your regular facial wash, pat dry (never rub), and wait for an hour. Don't apply any products during this time. After the hour, use a tissue to wipe your nose, cheeks, chin, and forehead, checking the tissue after wiping each area.

We should be able to categorize ourselves roughly into one of the following:

a. Oily—there will be oil transferred from all areas of the face onto the tissue.

b. Dry—tissue will possible pick up dry skin, flakes, but no oil whatsoever.

c. Normal—no oil or noticeable debris on tissue.

d. Combination—oil will be visible on the tissue from the T-zone: forehead, nose, and chin. The under eyes and cheek did not produce any oil.

19

In addition you might be:

e. Sensitive—you will most likely be aware of this already if you have allergies/reactions and general sensitivity such as redness or blotchiness. The products and regime you choose should be mindful of this.

There are three basic tenants to your skin care regime. How complicated you make it depends on how much work your skin type needs, but you will most likely find that contrary to your instincts, the less you play with your face, the better it will respond.

1. Cleanse—cleansing removes dirt, makeup, oil, and pollution from our environments.

2. Exfoliate—exfoliation reveals new skin cells and sheds old ones for that "glowy" look.

3. Moisturize—moisturizers keep skin cells healthy and strong, and using an SPF15 moisturizer daily will also prevent wrinkles and sun damage. Moisturize after showering or washing your face, when the face is damp but not wet.

NOTE: *Many people also include toning into their regime, but it is generally thought that this extra step is unnecessary unless you have oily skin and/or severe blackheads. Toners are supposed to make your pores look smaller - something a good moisturizer should do- and remove traces of makeup and dirt, something a decent cleanser should do. Therefore this extra step is not needed unless you have excessive oil. In this case, use it three times a week maximum, and look for a non-alcohol based one (this will dry out your skin).*

TIP: *Always replace lids and caps and avoid excess exposure to air and sunlight. Exposure to both of these things breaks down antioxidants and reduces the effectiveness of your products.*

What's The Hype About Exfoliation?

Our skin renews itself around 1,000 times during our lifetime, so there are plenty of opportunities to develop your dream dermis! New skin cells move to the surface of the skin every 3-4 weeks, and dry cells are supposed to shed, but some need that extra encouragement to leave! Exfoliation should be done 1-3 times a week (depending on skin type, see above) to help expose the new fresher, cleaner layer of skin cells.

As well as encouraging regeneration, moisturizers will be much more effective after exfoliation due to their ability to penetrate better into the skin. Exfoliation is great any time you have a special occasion or party but are feeling tired and worn out—it can turn around lifeless, dull skin and give it back some oxygen!

Reading Ingredient Labels

It may seem like a lot of work, but if you have any kind of skin problem (dryness, oiliness, sensitivity), reading the ingredients listed on cosmetic labels is as important as reading the food labels if you have food allergies or intolerances. Just write down a few ingredients to avoid and keep them in your purse or on your phone for easy reference while you shop. I will cover some of the important ones to look out for over the next few pages.

Now that you know your - skin type, let's take a closer look at what each one means.

Oily

Oily skin tends to be thicker than other types with larger pores. If your skin is oily, it is producing too much sebum (that's oil to you and me.)

The problem with oil is that it clogs up pores and this causes blackheads, whiteheads and acne. Oily skin needs more care and attention than the other skin types; therefore, cleansing is a crucial part of your skincare routine in order to avoid blockages and blackheads.

To find the perfect cleanser for oily skin, look for one that is oil-rich (ironic huh!), and use gel cleansers instead of milky ones. Many people with oily skin are afraid to moisturize, as they are reluctant to add more products to their skin. But oily skin can be dehydrated too (remember moisturizer is adding moisture, not oil), so do moisturize, albeit it with small amounts of product.

Exfoliation should be done 2-3 times a week as oily skin is most likely not sensitive. Use a granular exfoliating product and focus on your T-zone—the nose and forehead—where blackheads are most likely to make an appearance.

A few times a week after cleansing, exfoliating, and moisturizing, take a damp cotton pad and add toner. Run this across your T-zone. Toner closes your pores, which have been opened up during the cleansing process, particularly by warm water. The addition of a non-alcohol based toner should give your pores a smaller profile and your face a more even texture.

Ingredients to avoid for oily skin: Mineral Oil, Isopropyl Palmitate, Cocoa Butter, Lanolin, Isopropyl Myristate, Coconut Oil, Petrolatum, Paraffin.

Recommended Products for Oily Skin

Cleanser: *Look for gel cleansers that absorb excess oils—great for oily skin.*

Try Neutrogena's Wash-Away Gel Cleanser, $7.99; Clarins Prifying Cleansing Gel for Oily Skin $26; Shiseido Pureness Cleansing Gel $25

Exfoliator: *A grainy one is best, imagine the consistency of sand rather than beads.*

Try OLAY Definitely Pore Redefining Scrub, $9.99

Moisturizer: *Try an oil-free lightweight gel over thick creamy moisturizers.*

Try Neutrogena's Oil-free Moisturizer SPF 15, $10; Clinique Dramatically Different Moisturizing Gel, $24; Shiseido Pureness Moisturizing Gel, $24

Face Mask—*Clay-type masks are the best for oily skin.*

St. Ives Mineral Clay Firming Mask, $5; Laura Mercier Deep Cleansing Clay Mask $32.

Dry

Dry skin has less sebum (oil) than is desirable, and this results in the skin flaking, which often gets worse in cold weather. The skin can feel tight and uncomfortable after washing or showering, as if it is thirsty for moisture—and indeed dry skin does need extra moisture. Let moisturizer sink in for 5 minutes after the first application, and if need be, apply a second layer.

NOTE: *Dry skin should not be confused with dehydrated skin. Dry skin is a skin type while dehydrated skin is the state skin is in. Dry skin is lacking in oils, while dehydrated skin is in need of moisture!*

Avoid products that contain alcohol because it strips the skin of much-needed moisture, and all products used on dry skin should be sulfate-free. Formulas with sulfate in them (especially Sodium Lauryl Sulphate), causes products to foam up nicely, but they will leave skin dry and flaky by stripping the skin of the oils it needs.

TIP: *When bathing, use shower gel over an old-fashioned bar of soap, which is incredibly drying on the skin.*

At night after cleansing, use an oil to massage into skin (lavender and frankincense are good choices).

Your diet needs more oils—the good kind not greasy fries! Try oily fish or omega supplements, olive oil, safflower oil (the ultimate moisturizer from within!) and try to consume lots of water.

Recommended Products for Dry Skin

Cleanser: *Use a rich, creamy, or milk cleansers to cleanse the face morning and night.*

Try: Cetaphil Gentle Skin Cleanser, $7.99: Clinique Comforting Cream Cleanser, $18.50; Lancome Confort Galatee Cleansing Milk, $30.

Exfoliator: *Aim to exfoliate twice a week, using an exfoliator with beads rather than one with fine grains.*

Try: Clinique Gentle Exfoliator, $16.50; Demologica Gentle Cream Exfoliant, - $30.

Moisturizer: *Use a moisturizer with oils, and those specially designed for dry skin.*

Try: Eucerin's Facial moisturizer with SPF 30, $10. Aveeno Ultra-Calming Daily Moisturizer SPF 15, $16, Dr. HauschkaQuince Day Cream, $35.

Face Mask *- Hydration is key.*

Try: Phytomins Hydrating Face Mask - $9.99

Normal

If you fall into this category, you're a lucky bride -to–be!

So-called "'normal'" skin has a proper balance of oil, resulting in a fine, even texture. The pores are very small and barely visible. This skin type needs little care and very little make-up. The treatment of normal skin should be gentle and minimal to avoid causing an imbalance of oil production.

The only problem normal skin-types may have is associated with hormonal changes and stress— mostly pre-menstruation or after a late night where the occasional pimples are not uncommon. In addition, there might be premature aging around the eyes due to the lack of oil here. For this reason, eye cream should be an essential part of your everyday routine. (See page 37 for a note on eye creams)

A moisturizer might be necessary if you live in a dry climate or feel the need for it. However, if you find that it causes breakouts, stop using it! You are blessed enough to have skin that knows what to do without much guidance or interference from you, so roll with it!

Recommended Products for Normal Skin

Cleanser: *Cetaphil Gentle Skin Cleanser, $7.99; Phisoderm Deep Cleaning Cream Cleanser for normal to dry skin, $5; Laura Mercier One-Step Cleanser, $35.*

Exfoliator: *St. Ives Swiss Formula Apricot Scrub Blemish and Blackhead Control, $7.25.*

Moisturizer: *OLAY complete care daily UV cream, $7.99; L'Oreal Dermo-Expertise Active Daily Moisture Lotion SPF 15, $9; Clarins Hydration-Plus Moisture Lotion, $40.*

Face Mask*: A face mask for normal skin is optional. If you do choose to use one, a radiance-enhancing or deep cleansing masks are your best choices.*

Combination

Combination skin has both oily and dry areas split up roughly on the T-zone and the cheeks.

The most common combination type is an oily T-zone and dry cheeks, but the reverse is also possible.

Because the two areas of skin have different tendencies, they should be treated differently. However, the best way is to primarily treat the dominant skin type while paying attention to the other area.

1. **Oily combo**—gel cleansers, regular exfoliation, moisturize.

2. **Dry combo**—rich milk cleansers and oil rich moisturizers.

See the Oily and Dry sections above.

Sensitive

Sensitive skin refers to skin that reacts to environments, weather, and products in an unfavorable way, as well as a tendency for skin conditions such as eczema and rosacea. This skin type is fairly easy to recognize—it may be made obvious by tiny broken capillaries that lie across the cheeks, or an allergy/ sensitivity to products. If you are likely to flush red when you drink wine or eat spicy foods, this can also be a sign of sensitive skin.

The best advice for those with sensitive skin is to be really careful when using new products. Always patch-test these products for 24 hours before you go ahead and use them. To do this, take a small amount of the product and place it behind the ear, then don't wash this area for an entire 24 hours. If after this time period there is no irritation or flare up, it should be safe to use the product elsewhere on the body. You should also look to use fragrance-free products (this is not the same as unscented; check specifically for the words "fragrance-free") as well as hypoallergenic ones.

Those with sensitive skin should avoid using really hot water, and instead stick with lukewarm water when washing the face or bathing. Your cleanser should be a milky/creamy one as opposed to a gel one, and when it comes to exfoliation, once a week should be ample. Use a creamy, dry exfoliator, which differs from a regular one in that it needs to be applied in a dry space—not in the shower or bath. Allow it to dry, and rather than rinsing it off, rub it away with your ring finger. With it will come all of the dead skin and build up (particularly around your nose), leaving a nice layer of fresh glowy skin!

Using a dry exfoliator is much gentler on the skin and should minimize the irritation felt by sensitive skin.

Those with sensitive skin might feel more comfortable using mineral makeup (such as BareEscentuals) since their products are often free of pesky chemical ingredients that sensitive skin reacts badly to. See page 57 for more information on mineral makeup.

Ingredients to avoid for sensitive skin: Triethanolamine, any products that don't list the ingredients on the label (some are permitted by the FDA not to do so), any labels that simply state "and other ingredients."

Sensitive Skin Tip!

As a side note, those with sensitive skin should consider using a mild laundry detergent formulated especially for those with sensitive skin. A friend told me that this has made a huge difference to the comfort of her clothes and underwear, and additionally her face was less reactive because the towels she used to dry her face were no longer causing irritation.

Blackheads, Whiteheads, Acne

Time to talk about these monsters. To understand how to avoid/get rid of acne, we should look at what acne is. Acne develops when the pores of our skin become blocked by "sebum," the oil on our skin.

What kind of skin you have—oily, dry or normal—will determine the kind of spots you might be prone to developing.

Blimmin' Blackheads

That lovely friend of ours, the blackhead, appears when sebum, along with dead skin cells, blocks the skin's pores. The pore is open and clogged. Because the pore is open, the gunk reacts with oxygen and the oxidization results in a black color.

While it is tempting to squeeze out those blackheads, it is a risky endeavor since this will only encourage the dirt to spread into nearby pores and across your face. The best way to get rid of this excess oil and dead skin cells is to exfoliate regularly. You really will notice a dramatic improvement in your blackheads as you slough away gunk and dead skin cells through exfoliation. Your pores will also appear much smaller.

If you have really stubborn blackheads that have been present for a while, invest in a facial and have this gunk professionally removed since exfoliation might not be enough. You can read more about professional facials on page 31.

Wicked Whiteheads

A whitehead forms in a similar way as a blackhead—excess oil and dead skin cells clog the pore. However, unlike blackheads, the surface of the skin is closed. This results in a white surface, since the gunk has not yet been oxidized, and is slightly less unattractive than the dark surface of the blackhead. Again, exfoliation is your friend. In addition, a trained skin expert can rid you of these unwanted guests without spreading infection, causing an aggravated spot or scarring.

Recommended products for ridding yourself of blackheads and whiteheads:

Cleanse: *Biore Warming Anti-Blackhead Cream Cleanser ($7.99)*

Exfoliate: *Clean & Clear Blackhead Eraser Scrub ($6.49)*

Take serious action!: *Biore Deep Cleansing Pore Strips ($10.49 for a pack of 14)*

Red Acne—Pimples

For those of you whose skin falls into "oily" or those who have parts of the face that fit this description (combination), the excess oil does more damage than just clogging the pores. The bacteria that otherwise live quite normally on our skin (yes, even yours madam!) thrive in these oily conditions. In fact, they cause all sorts of mayhem along the way. Getting drunk on this excess oil, bacteria breeds and increases in size and quantity quite rapidly.

Clogged pores collapse under the pressure of too much reproduction and cause inflammation that results in not-so-attractive red, hot, engorged look. Here, the clogged pores are too far along to benefit from exfoliation, and doing so might only exacerbate your oil production, damage any broken skin, and spread bacteria around the face. So how should we handle these red devils?

What You Can Do To Keep Your Skin Clear—Preventative Measures

* **Change Your Pillowcase Regularly.** There are so many bacteria on your pillowcase, from your hair, hands, face, dribble... If you are prone to breakouts this is a great first step.

* **Keep Your Phone Clean.** If you notice you are breaking out on one side on your face, this may be why.

* **Keep Your Hands Off Your Face** as much as possible. The average person touches their face 18 times an hour - thats a lot of grime being transferred across your face!

* **Always Remove Your Makeup Before Bed** (Yes, always! I'm wise to your game!)

* Avoid the spreading of bacteria and thus sidestepping clogged pores - by **Washing Your Makeup Brushes Regularly.** Use a facial soap or shampoo, rinse them well, and let them dry naturally overnight.

* When choosing a **Makeup Remover, Non-Oily Pads Are Best**. (*Try Jason Naturals Quick Clean Non-Oily Makeup Remover,* $5.50 for 75 pads). As I so delightfully explained, excess oil is not our friend when it comes to clear skin. Additionally, non-oily pads will cause less irritation to sensitive skin and are more suitable for contact lens wearers. They also won't damage the delicate skin around the eyes.

✳ Try using **Mineral Makeup**. It is an excellent alternative to regular makeup as it sits on the skin rather than sinking into the pores. Some women complain that it is more obvious that you are wearing makeup because of this, but in terms of skin care, mineral makeup allows the skin to breathe and doesn't congest the pores.

To Facial or Not?

Despite what you might have heard from the industry "experts," professional facials are, for most of us, a non-essential indulgence. If you are wondering whether or not you need to start having facials, know that it is a luxury rather than a necessity. A fine skincare program can take place at home.

See below for an example of an at-home facial, suitable for oily, dry, and combination skin.

When You Should Have a Professional Facial

• *To learn the basics of skincare for future reference and get a professional's advice on your skin.*

• *If you have tried at-home facials and have stubborn blackheads that just don't want to go anywhere, please get a professional extraction rather than forcing them out yourself. Sometimes those finicky blackheads have been sitting there for so long they just don't want to leave.*

• *As a stress-reliever. Similar to massage, facials can have a relaxing effect, produce short-term improvements in our skin, and make us feel special.*

If you do opt to have facials, just make sure that you have your final one at least two weeks before the wedding. Facials can encourage short-term breakouts and cause redness as bacteria is brought to the skin's surface. You will be red and blotchy, and should avoid wearing any kind of product for a few hours afterwards, so save facials for a night in!

At-Home Facial (once a week)

Set one day a week for your at-home facial; see the last section for product recommendations for your skin type

1. **Cleanse**

Remove creams, sunscreen, makeup, and dirt with a cleanser.

2. **Exfoliate**

Using a circular motion and plenty of warm water (unless you are using a dry type), rub the exfoliator into your hand to warm it up, and then apply it onto your face. Concentrate on the nose or anywhere you have blackheads or build up. Rinse off well.

3. **Steam Bath**

Place a large bowl of steaming hot water on a table, and bend over placing your face above it. Then, place a towel over the back of your head and drape it over the bowl so that all of the steam from the water is trapped underneath the towel. After 10 minutes, the pores should have softened and opened. You can an extraction tool or two pieces of cotton pads on either side of offending blackheads to coax them out. Never use your fingers to do this no matter how tempting it might be!

Making Changes to Your Skin From the Inside

* **Hydration**—if you are not getting enough water, this will show clearly on your skin. See page 104 for more reasons on why water is great, but just know that it is the one thing that will make a huge difference to your skin.

* **Your diet**—you might have food intolerances that show up on your skin, or you may know of some foods or drink that trigger your breakouts. While you might not be willing to give up the foods that cause your breakouts in the long run (Alcohol, caffeine, nuts, sugar and greasy food are all common culprits) you might want to make a conscious effort to avoid them during this month.

* **Vitamins C, E, and calcium** are very important for your skin's beauty. Make sure to take your vitamins! (see page 116)

* **Omega 3** moisturizes the skin from the inside out and provides you with the type of oils that are beneficial to your skin. Cold water fish, flaxseeds, walnuts, and green veggies are all great sources. See more in the health section on page 108 and 109.

For information on 'Zits on your Day' & the 'Top 3 Pimple Calmers' see page 204

Minimizing Pores

The pore is a natural part of the skins make-up; it is where the hair follicle is rooted, and where oil and sweat reach the surface and leave the skin. In some cases, the oil does not leave the pore effectively and ends up "plugging" the skin, resulting in blackheads, which draws attention to the pore and temporarily enlarges them. This is why a proper cleansing and exfoliating regime is crucial!

Unfortunately, the size of your pores is fixed genetically and cannot be changed. If however, the size of your pores is causing you grief, there are few things you can do to change the appearance of their size. When pores are free from oil, they will appear much smaller.

1. Remove current grime in the pore (blackhead). Use an exfoliant, steam bath or professional extraction.

2. Reduce oil levels.

3. Draw the pores closed after cleansing and exfoliating using cold water and an astringent toner.

Glowing Advice from Greece!

As well as being a great healthy snack and good for your digestive system, yogurt is used as a topical beauty treatment in Greece. It is naturally full of lactose, proteins, vitamins and minerals, and yogurt is placed directly on the skin and used as a solution to treat sunburn and other skin problems. You can also add honey, which has a natural anti-bacterial effect to make a great, natural facemask!

Bacne

Bacne is the endearing term used to describe acne on the back, chest, and other body parts. It can be the cause of much frustration and unhappiness, since not only does it not look too cool, it can cause itchiness and discomfort. The skin on the back is much thicker than on the face, and pores are also larger here, so it can be harder to deal with. One of the main causes of bacne is sweat. Bacteria love to feast on it, and when you sweat, the body produces oil; therefore, it is super important to not skip a shower post-workout!

Some rules to follow to avoid/get rid of bacne:

* Wash ASAP after a workout.

* Damp sweaty clothing is bacne's best friend—wear breathable cotton clothing as much as possible.

* Keep your bed sheets as clean as possible.

* Try not to shower more than once a day. This way you can avoid excessive oil production.

* Exfoliate regularly with a body scrub.

* Keep fabrics clean, especially your underwear. Obviously, this is especially important for your sports bra.

* Avoid carrying a backpack that will aggravate the situation.

* Try a medicated body wash with 2% salicylic acid. One of the most popular and talked about is *Neutrogena Body Clear Body Wash.*

* Tea tree oil in its various forms (body washes, wipes, sprays, and oils) can keep bacne under control by acting as a disinfectant and killing spot-causing bacteria.

Top 3 Treatments for Bacne

1. *Neutrogena Body Clear Body Wash $6-10 for 8.5oz*

2. *Neutrogena Acne Stress Control Power Cream Body Wash ~$8 for 8.5 oz*

3. *Tea tree cleansing wipes—The Body Shop. $12 for 25.*

TIP—*If you are using a medicated face wash, pay special attention not to get the medicated body wash on your face. Applying both may lead to over-medication and the ingredients in both may not be compatible, may dry out the skin or cause an unwanted reaction.*

Keeping Skin Young for Life

It's been a long day, you've had a late night, and you are just dying to crawl under your bed covers.

Stop! Not removing your makeup is one of the biggest crimes you can commit against your skin despite how tempting it can be. I know, I've been there too many times. But as well as being a leading cause of pimples, not washing off your makeup is also a wrinkle-causing offender. Like the sports brand says, *Just Do It!*.

Eye makeup—eye shadow, mascara, and particularly eye liner—can settle in the thin skin around your eyes and over time will result in fine lines. If fine wrinkles are already making an appearance, the good news is that they are not yet hard-set enough to be considered permanent. Unlike deep lines, fine wrinkles might not require too much time, effort, or money to get rid of them.

Here is a simple rule to keep wrinkles as far away as possible - the skin products you choose should contain three things:

1. Sunscreen of at least SPF 15 (this adds a barrier against sun damage.)

2. Peptides—these boost collagen production

3. Antioxidants—- these fight pollution, sun damage and other pollutants to the skin.

Top 3 Supplements to Prevent Aging

1. **Vitamin C**—An antioxidant that encourages collagen production

2. **Fish or Flaxseed Oil**—Contains essential Omega 3 fatty acids

3. **Coenzyme Q10**—An antioxidant that protects the skin, giving cells energy for reparation. One word of warning: when taking this supplement, you may notice a stimulating effect similar to that of coffee! Make sure to take it in the morning and don't pop one right before bed!

Humidifiers & Sun Protection

A humid atmosphere helps keep skin supple and wrinkle free, which explains why a lot of women living in Asia and other humid environments often have such young-looking skin. In drier climates, or if you have dry skin, it is advisable to humidify your room. If you don't have a humidifier, try placing a small dish filled with water in the room that you sleep in at night—this will add moisture to the air.

If you live in a hot climate, or even if you don't but you spend any amount of time outdoors, you should be religiously wearing sunscreen. Your sunscreen should be at least SPF 15 (I recommend higher), and check the label to ensure that it provides broad-spectrum UVA-UVB coverage. Remember, UV rays can penetrate through windows, car windscreens, and thin clothing, as well as persisting on cloudy days. It is best to think of your sunscreen as a moisturizer (or indeed choose a moisturizer with an SPF in it), and to apply it on a daily basis rather than only those days you know that you'll be lying on the beach or are consciously "catching some rays,"

Sun protection is the biggest step you can take to staying beautiful into old age. To make sure that your SPF protects from UVA & UVB, look for the ingredients titanium dioxide and zinc oxide on the label.

Eye Cream

Using an eye cream is recommended from your mid-late 20's, especially if your skin is dry. If you have oily skin, you might want to use a light gel rather than a cream to avoid oiliness.

37

Start using a serum if you want to get really serious about your war on wrinkles. Unlike eye creams, a good quality serum nourishes the dermal layer of the skin, the layer that provides firmness and elasticity, thus repairing the dermis and improving the skin's appearance.

Apply gel/cream/serum with your ring finger —this finger is less damaging to the thin skin around the eye as it is the weakest and naturally produces less pressure. Using this finger, gently apply pressure to various pressure points under the eye. Try not to pull the skin, and dab, do not rub. Don't take the product right up to the eyelashes, even if this is where your fine lines are showing. The skin will transport the product here naturally.

30 Day Regime for Clear Skin

- **Invest in a good sunscreen if you do not already own one.** *Use one with SPF 30 UVA and UVB. Also cover up and avoid sunlight from 10-2pm. This will not only protect you from aging, skin discoloration, but also acne breakouts (which won't show up until a week after sun exposure.)*

- *Avoid touching your face when possible.*

- *Determine your skin type (see page 19 to ensure that the products you own are appropriate for your skin type.)*

- *Exfoliate 1-3 times a week depending upon your skin type.*

- *Change your pillowcases regularly—moisturizers, creams, hair products, and sweat will transfer to your pillow over night.*

- *Perform an at-home facial if and when you need one.*

Tanning

> ## "THE WAY TO MAKE COACHES THINK YOU ARE IN SHAPE IN THE SPRING IS TO GET A TAN."
>
> ### WHITEY FORD

Assuming you are wearing a white dress on your big day (I'm just taking a wild guess here), a healthy tan can help prevent you from looking washed out if you are naturally fair-skinned. It can also give the appearance of looking slimmer and toned - fabulous!

However, a tan should not compromise your health, so don't put vanity in front of your risk of developing skin cancer. (Wow things just turned serious, sorry!). Thankfully, the dangers of tanning booths have been brought to our attention by the media in recent years and are facing increasing and much-needed regulations. The Obama administration recently imposed a 10% tanning tax, signaling that indoor tanning poses serious health risks.

It is really easy to ignore these warnings, but honestly, having a perma-tan from a tanning booth is not going to make you beautiful in 20 years time. I'm guessing that you enjoy it when you are having a good skin day now, and most likely you will want that in the future, too. In that case you are going to regret aging your skin and the sunspots that come with tanning.

The Dangers of Tanning Booths

It really is one of life's ironies that skin damage (what tanning is) is considered sexy. Possibly because tanned skin looks slimmer, hides imperfections easier and creates that image of being the fun-loving beach babe who parties by the coast.

Like most damaging things—cigarettes, alcohol, drugs—tanning can be addictive. The feel-good factor of being in the heat, the resulting golden glow, both make you want to go back for more. Tanning booth users often justify this addiction by claiming that tanning forms a protective barrier to protect them from natural sunlight. I have to tell you, this logic is BS.

Yes, tanning booths give off fewer UVB rays than natural sunlight. But they also give out 3 to 8 times more UVA rays than the sun. This leads to skin cancer (regular users have a 75% increased risk of developing melanoma, the deadly kind), eye damage, not to mention premature aging.

I know, I know, I'm preaching here. And I am a former sun-worshipper myself. At 21 I was dying to look older (people think its a compliment when they tell you you still look like you are in Junior High) —now I regret every minute of it. Now I am rocking the English rose look I was born with instead!

If the damage is already done, start wearing sunscreen and stay out of the sun during the peak hours (10-2). If you still use tanning booths, do yourself a huge favor and, stop. If you're addicted to the heat, take up hot yoga. If you are addicted to the tan, fake it. As a doctor-friend once told me, "titty-toasting is one of the worst things you can do for your long term health!"

UV Lowdown

There are two kinds of UV rays that we should protect our skin from.

UVB—*Short rays that hit the skin's surface. Think* **B for Burn.**

UVA—*Long, penetrating rays that go deep into the skin and damage the skin cells. Think* **A for Aging.**

Tip: Windows don't block out UVA. Wear sunscreen everyday even when you are driving in the car or sitting inside close to a window all day. The easiest way to do this is to choose makeup or a facial moisturizer with a minimum of SPF 15 built in.

What to Do if the Damage is Already Done

A recent, inconclusive, yet promising study, suggests that some vitamins may help to reduce the aging caused by sun exposure. Here is a list of those vitamins and where to find them:

Vitamin A—*Sweet Potatoes, Carrots, Mangoes, Spinach, Egg Yolk to name a few.*

Vitamin C—*Broccoli, Cauliflower, Kiwis, Strawberries, Oranges, Peppers, Greens, Lemon Juice, Papaya.*

Vitamin E—*Nuts, Tomatoes, Wheat Germ Oil, Sunflower Seeds, Spinach.*

The Safest—And Most Natural—Kind of Tan

Self-tanning is certainly the safest way to get some color, yet before making the mistake of looking like a pumpkin in your pics, be really careful about deciding whether to go with a fake bake or not. Some self-tanners are dramatically better than others; some work well on one skin type and will turn another into an oompa lumpa. I've sure learned the hard way.. high school. Oh and once in University. Oh and several times since... It's all about trial and error, so make sure you do some trial this month rather than having a *Sunny Delight* style error on your wedding day.

Spray Tan

For an all-over tan without having to get your hands messy or worry about covering those difficult to reach areas.

Spray tanning uses a spray-on form of DHA (dihydroxyacetone—phew!), which darkens the outer layer of the skin until the skin renews itself (basically until it falls off). DHA is approved by the FDA and is regarded as a safe alternative to sun exposure. (It is also what makes self-tan smell funky). Depending on your age and skin, results will last around one week. You can choose the strength of the tanning solution depending on your desired result and your natural skin tone. You should really only go one… maximum two…tones darker than that.

Spray tanning is performed in a booth in most cases, but in some salons—and if you are not shy—you can have someone perform your spray tan (known as air-brush tanning). This option allows you to specify the areas that you want extra attention paying to, and makes sure that all angles can be tackled thoroughly.

Pointers for a Spray Tan

Before you go:

* Exfoliate

The fresher your skin is, the longer the results will last. The evening before your spray tan, exfoliate all over (paying special attention to knees and elbows, which will absorb the color more easily) and moisturize well. Doing both of these things will reduce the chances of uneven, blotchy coloring.

* Remove unwanted hair

If you usually shave or wax, do so before your spray treatment, not afterwards. Both remove dead skin cells, which will cause color fading.

✱ Don't put on deodorant, cosmetics, or perfume the day of the spray tan

You want to be in your most natural state! Wearing any of these things can cause blotchiness.

✱ Wear loose and dark clothing

Wear loose, dark clothing to and from the salon to avoid the formula transferring to your clothes. If possible, go bra-less and wear old underwear.

After the Spray Tan

✱ Wait six hours before showering. This will help extend the life of your tan.

✱ Avoid exercise or sweating.

✱ Moisturize after each shower you take for the next week.

TIP: *To locate a spray tan salon near you, head to* **http://bit.ly/ bD9RYj** *and type in your zip code.*

Fake Tan

If you choose to perform a fake tan at home, there are some important points you should keep in mind.

1. Exfoliate—this is the number one way to avoid streaking.

2. You should take special care to rub it in, and in order to do this, don't over-apply (or apply too little).

3. Pay special attention to your knees, elbows, hands, feet, and neck where any mistakes will be the most noticeable. (Particularly the tops of your feet and around your toes where skin is dry and tends to absorb unevenly).

4. Be sure to let it dry. This can take anywhere from 5-15 minutes, so apply it when you are not in a rush.

5. Wash your hands thoroughly (unless you opt to use gloves). Fake tan tends to get under your nails and between the fingers, which looks pretty gross.

TIP—*Use a makeup sponge when applying fake tan to your face, hands, and feet for more even coverage.*

A lot of self-tanners have that strong, unmistakable self-tanner smell, but some do come with less powerful odors. One product that is less stinky is *Jergens Natural Glow* ($8.99). It is cheap, effective, and it doesn't smell so bad.

NOTE: *Be sure to avoid sun exposure for 8-12 hours after fake tan application. Two ingredients in fake tan—DHA and erythulose—cause a rise in the generation of free radicals when exposed to UV light, which increases the damaging effects of the sun to your skin. What an unfortunate irony!*

Slow-Tanning Moisturizers

Slow-Tanning Moisturizers combine a daily moisturizer with a low-strength self tan. Thus, no messy streaks, no missed-a-bit patches, and no uneven tones. You still have to carefully choose the right shade (they may come in different levels) to avoid that orange look and the desired look will take longer to achieve. There is less room for error though. As with fake tans, make sure to wash your hands and nails thoroughly after use, as they can stain and make nails appear fungal! Alternatively, you can try using surgical gloves for application.

A slow-tanning moisturizer I recommend is *Nivea Body Firming Moisturizer, Sun-Kissed for Light to Medium Skin or Medium to Dark Skin* ($7.49 for 250ml).

30 Day Regime for the Perfect Tan

- *Use a slow-tanning moisturizer or a fake tan mixed with moisturizer in the weeks leading up to the wedding. A nice tan should develop within 3-5 days of application. If you feel that it is getting too dark, skip a day and control the depth of the tan this way. You will soon get a grip on how long it takes to develop the shade of your choice.*

- *If you are braving the spray tan, **book it for two days before the wedding.** On day 2 it will reach its darkest color, and by day 3 it will have settled to the perfect tint. After that you run the risk of it fading or flaking. Make sure to have a trial a few weeks before the wedding to test out the depth and longevity of the shade/tan you are going to try.*

Makeup and Cosmetics

"WOMEN HAVE TWO WEAPONS—COSMETICS AND TEARS."

COCO CHANEL

Makeup on the Day

Goodness, where to start! The choice these days is mind-boggling, and I for one am baffled as to where they get these ideas for new mascara brushes. Will they ever run out?! There are makeup categories that never even used to exist, so it is not surprising that you might need some professional help to walk you through it.

There are a few options for the makeup on your day:

1. You can hire a professional

2. Ask a friend who is good with cosmetics

3. Or if you feel confident enough, you can do it yourself. By now, you have probably already decided which option to go with.

1. The Professional Route

Using a professional makeup artist is a good idea for many reasons. Perhaps you are unfamiliar with makeup don't own many cosmetics, or simply aren't confident enough to create the look that you want. If you don't own the makeup that you need, hiring a makeup artist makes sense financially rather than running out and spending a $100 on makeup that you might never use again. Bridal makeup is different than regular makeup—it

has to last all day (and night!), needs to be "camera-friendly," and for this reason, it needs to be slightly heavier than you would otherwise want to wear it.

Your Professional Trial Tips

Try to schedule a makeup trial beforehand; this helps you and the makeup artist achieve the look you want. You can time this with your engagement shoot if you are having one, or another special night.

* Take a digital camera along and make sure that the result looks good on camera too!

* Take your wedding jewelry and headpiece to get a good balance between the makeup and your accessories.

* Wear a white/ivory loose top so you can check the entire look against the color of your dress. Wearing a button down shirt will mean that you can change after the trial without worrying about getting it on your clothes.

* A picture speaks a thousand words! Take pictures from magazines, online, or photos to help your artist understand the look you are hoping to achieve.

* When practicing, consider the lighting. A daytime wedding should be practiced in daytime lighting (especially if it is outside), and an evening should be practiced under reception hall level lighting.

A Lesson Learned

Exactly three days before my wedding, I called my makeup artist to confirm our trial the next day, only for him to tell me that he wasn't going to be able to do my wedding makeup after all because of a 'family commitment'. I had booked him four months in advance and was so angry at his unprofessionalism. This was the most bridezilla-ish I got – I was distraught!

In the end things worked out great, and a friend of a friend stepped in to save the day. The moral of the story is not to freak you out! It's that a) always be sure to double-check appointments with your vendors ahead of time, and b) things go wrong in the week before the wedding. But they will always turn out alright in the end, I promise!

2. What You Need To Know If You Are Going DIY

If you are planning to do your own makeup, take advantage of the sales people at the cosmetic counters in department stores to learn some tricks. Pay close attention to the products they use on you and how they apply each one. Don't feel pressured to buy everything they use! (See page 58 for more advice on this.)

It is important to know the difference between everyday makeup and bridal makeup. Bridal makeup will be heavier, longer lasting, and should try to avoid anything that is going to create shine or reflection in your pictures.

I consulted Los Angeles-based makeup artist, Elaine Chou of EChou Studio, to share with us the step-by step secrets of perfect, long-lasting bridal makeup.

Step-by-Step Guide to DIY Makeup

Moisturize, Prime, Foundation, Blush, Powder, Eyes, Lips, Check!

1. Firstly, **moisturize.** Always apply lotion to your face to create a smooth base on which to work on. If you plan to use powder later (which you should), a lotion with SPF 15 or above can be used, since the powder will take the shine out of the SPF. If you are not going to use a powder, avoid using a lotion containing sunscreen.

2. **Prime**—A primer such as *Smashbox Photo Finish Foundation Primer* (Sephora, $36) will inhibit the production of oils and thus prevent makeup from sliding off. In addition, it will stop the skin from absorbing foundation by creating a barrier between the skin and makeup, thus enabling it to last longer.

3. **Foundation**—Apply foundation across the whole face, making sure to blend it in at the hairline and neck. The coverage should be heavier around the under eye area, sides of the nose and mouth, and over any pimples or blemishes. For a detailed explanation on how to apply foundation, see the section "The Foundations of Foundation" on page 54.

4. **Cheeks**—Elaine suggests using a cream blush rather than a powder, since it is easier to blend into the skin, more natural-looking, and stays on for longer. MAC Blushcreme in Ladyblush ($19.50) fits most skin tones. Use your fingers or a sponge to apply, either at a 45-degree angle or in a straight line, across the cheek.

Blush

Applying blush at a 45 degree angle will create a more dramatic look, forcing your features to stand out. Blush straight across the cheek will create a younger "cuter" look. To apply blush at a 45 degree angle, smile in the mirror and find the apple of your cheek. Blend the blush upwards and out from here, toward the temple.

If using powder blush, don't use the small, square brush that accompanies a compact blush—invest in a good, blush brush to get more even coverage and avoid the streaky look! Powder blush works well for some people, but is not advisable for those with dry skin. Try a cream one instead.

Blush fades fast— so keep some in your bag so that you can re-touch.

5. Set the look so far with a **translucent powder**. The powder won't change the color you have achieved since it is translucent. Elaine recommends using MAC Prep & Prime Transparent Finishing Powder ($22) and using a large brush to sweep it across the face gently.

6. **Eyebrows**—time to fill in any sparse areas and create the perfect shape. If you have hair to work with here, it is best to use an eye shadow color that suits you (usually one shade lighter than your natural color), and a brush to fill in the gaps and enhance the shape. If you don't have much hair, a brow pencil is more suitable since eye shadow will not be able to cling on to your skin. Using a sealant, such as *She Laq* from Benefit ($30), will ensure that the eye pencil stays on all day. (This sealant can also be used to hold lip liner, lipstick, and eye shadow in place.)

7. **Eye shadow**—Use a primer as your base to ensure that eye shadow stays put. Elaine shares with us two looks you can achieve with your eyes:

The Cat Eye

1. Use a white/ivory color eyeshadow to highlight the area under the eyebrow.

2. Use a gold eye shadow on the lid, starting off lightly in the inner corner and fading into a darker gold or brown as you work towards the outer corner.

3. Close to the upper lash line, use an eyeliner to draw a line that extends all the way past the outer corner of the lid. This will achieve the feline look, making the eyes look wider.

4. Use mascara to really accentuate the lashes in the outer corner. Apply several coats to individual lashes, and make sure that these get great coverage.

The Round Eye

1. Use a white or ivory shadow to highlight under the brow.

2. On your eyelid use whatever color you wish to work with, be it blue, green, purple and so on. The area closer to the eye should use a darker shade of this color, and it should fade upwards.

3. Use eyeliner to make the eye appear rounder by making the eyeliner thicker in the middle part of the eye and thinner in the inner and outer edges. This creates an illusion of roundness. Longer faux eyelashes can be applied in the middle part of the eye to achieve this same effect.

8. **Eyeliner**—depending on the eye shape you wish to achieve (see above), draw a thick line close to the lash. Liquid eyeliner is best, even though it is generally too heavy for everyday wear; it is suitable for bridal makeup since the heavy eyelashes will offset it.

MAC Liquid Last Liner in Point Black (<u>www.MACcosmetics.com</u>, department stores, ($16.50) is a waterproof liner that won't budge even when you cry tears of joy!

9. Eyelashes—**Using an eyelash curler**, curl your lashes to open up the eyes. Curl them in three different places—the root, midway up, and near the tip. Use the curler very gently, with a light press. Clamping heavily will weaken the hair and contribute to lash loss. If you plan to use faux eyelashes, see page 82 for tips on how to apply them.

   ❋ Mascara—If you are not wearing faux eyelashes, **use a waterproof mascara** to finish off the eyes. Start close to the root of the eyelash, and using a zig-zag motion move toward the ends of the lashes. To get the illusion of wide, almond-shaped eyes as well as high cheekbones, drag the wand of your mascara horizontally outward and upward in slow motions. Repeat this two times.

10. **Lips**—Apply the color of your choice to the lips. Lipliner is optional here. Lipsticks will photograph darker than they look in the mirror, so try to stay soft. Neutral colors—nudes, soft browns, rose—are more flattering than brighter colors.

TIP—*Blue-based hues in lipsticks will help teeth appear whiter!*

11. **Final check**—make sure the coverage under the eyes is heavy enough, if not, touch up now. Re-apply some cheek color if necessary, and finish with a final dusting of powder. You're all set!

The Foundations of Foundation and Concealer

Foundation is a whole science of its own. Elaine blew me away with her detailed explanations of what type of foundation to wear and how to wear it! Here are her top tips:

While liquid foundation is sufficient for everyday use, the coverage is simply not good enough for bridal makeup. On the other hand, cake foundation has great coverage, but is too heavy for some skin types and may cause the fine lines around the eyes and mouth to be made more obvious, especially when you smile (which you will be doing a lot of!)

Therefore, mixing a liquid and cake foundation together is a way of getting the best of both worlds—great coverage without being too heavy. Use a makeup palette (or if you don't own one, a CD—either side of the disc will do!) to mix the two together until you have reached a consistency and color that you are happy with. This can be tested on the jaw line, or chest (which generally receives the same amount of sunlight as the face, unlike the neck which is shaded and may be an unrepresentative color).

To create a nice contour so that your face looks slimmer and more defined, apply foundation one shade darker on the outer rim of your face. Obviously make sure this blends nicely with the foundation that you use for the main part of the face.

Concealer can be then be applied to any areas necessary. The coverage should be heavier around the corners of the nose and mouth, the under eyes, and on any blemishes. To apply concealer, use a brush to dab it on in one direction. Don't go back and forth with it—you'll be undoing all your hard work! Blend it in with light touches of your ring finger.

When choosing a concealer or foundation, it is important to consider what undertone your skin has. All women have a pink or yellow undertone, regardless of their skin color. The easiest way to check this is to look at the color of the veins in your wrist. If they are blue, you have a pink undertone. If the veins are greenish, you have a yellow undertone.

Most of the major brands take these undertones into consideration. One of the reasons MAC has earned such cult-status is because of their wide variety of tones and shades to choose from. They separate their concealers and foundations into four categories—W for Warm (pink tone), C for Cool (yellow tone), NW for Neutral Warm and NC for Neutral Cool. A MAC assistant can help you choose the correct tone and shade for your skin tone.

The MAC concealer Elaine recommends is *Select Cover Up Corrector*, (10 ml for $16.50); the cake foundation of choice is *MAC Studio Tech*, ($29.50) and the liquid foundation she recommends mixing it with is *MAC Select Liquid Foundation* ($26).

Professional Or DIY—Things To Remember Either Way

* A softer look is better. You want the groom to see you, just more polished than usual, and not an entirely different woman walking toward him down the aisle!

* Avoid "trends" such as overly smokey eyes. You will be looking at these pictures for years to come.

* Exfoliate, starting three weeks beforehand. Makeup looks better on a smooth surface. This includes the lips - use an old toothbrush to remove any dead skin.

* Moisturize. Especially the face and lips, for the same reason as above.

* If trying new products, do so two weeks beforehand, and no closer, to the wedding date.

* Find inspirational pics in magazines to imitate.

* Employ a bridesmaid to check your makeup throughout the day—carry your lipstick, perfume and so on.

* Wear waterproof. Think you won't cry? You most likely will! (For happy reasons hopefully). Use waterproof mascara as well as waterproof foundation and eyeliner.

* Keep shimmer light and natural. Don't apply too much and only in one area. It can add to your natural glow and look beautiful, but if worn badly it may make your face look oily or sweaty.

* Start with less and build up to more—be it foundation, blush or eye makeup. It is always easier to add more than to take it away; this can end in a horrible mess.

Tattoo/Scar/ Birthmark Cover Up

If you have a tattoo, scar, or birthmark that shows with your dress, you may want to leave it on show as a part of "you". Check out Tattoodbride.com

Alternatively if you choose to cover it up, there are several options available. Try the following sites to see pictures of each product and learn more about how each one works:

Cover Up Kits

* Mehron tattoo cover up – **www.stageandtheatermakeup.com/mhtattoo.htm**

* Dermablend – **www.dermablend.com**

* Tattoo Camo – **www.tattoocamo.com**

* David's Bridal Tattoo Cover Up Kit—Available in store or at **www.davidsbridal.com**

For scars—Try "Invicible Scars" (**http://www.inviciblescars.com/**) for surgery scars, accidental scars, acne scars, as well as pigmentation and age spots.

Notes On Using Tattoo Cover-up Kits

It is essential that you do a trial before the day. If possible, ask for samples of the product you are interested in before ordering so that you can practice without dropping any money if the results don't satisfy you and can find the correct color for your skin tone.

The results of tattoo cover-up kits will depend on how big the tattoo is and how strong the colors are.

When practicing—apply, let it dry for ten minutes and then use a powder to set it.

Choosing a Sunscreen To Wear On The Day

As mentioned in the cosmetic section, choose a lotion with an SPF for your face, but be sure to use a powder to set it - to avoid shine in your photographs. If you choose to use sunscreen on other parts of your body— chest, arms, and neck—choose an oil-free product to avoid shine/reflection. Sunscreen formulas that contain zinc are non-greasy and non-irritating; this is great news for acne sufferers who avoid sunscreen for fear of causing flare-ups.

Mineral Makeup

If you suffer from sensitive skin or breakout frequently, mineral makeup might be a good choice for you. Free of perfumes, alcohols, and preservatives, mineral makeup is less likely to cause allergic reactions or irritation (that's hypoallergenic in posh terms).

Additionally, mineral makeup is non-comedogenic (it won't block your pores and contribute to acne).

Try one of the following popular brands;

* **BareEscentuals** (www.bareescentuals.com, Sephora, BareEscentuals store nationwide.)

57

* **Sheer Cover** (www.sheercover.com)

* **Colorescience** (Visit www.colorescience and enter your zipcode to locate your nearest store.)

* **Youngblood** (Visit www.ybskin.com to find your nearest store.)

Cosmetic Counters —To Purchase Or Not To Purchase?

Makeup counters in department stores are a great place to receive the hands-on, see-it-feel-it experience necessary before you drop a bomb on something new. While many counters offer a "free" consultation, whether or not there is a purchase requirement or not is a difficult piece of etiquette to address.

I find that the best method is to ask straight-up what their store policy is, and then if I don't intend to purchase, but are genuinely interested in learning about their products, being honest about it makes both the consultant and I far more relaxed. I explain that I'm not looking to purchase today but will shop around, take notes, and am looking to purchase in the near future. Many consultants realize that an on-the-spot purchase is not as valuable as the word-of-mouth marketing that you will no doubt give them from your makeover. And if you tell them you are looking for makeup for your wedding, they are more than often very happy to help.

Many of us (myself included!) find department store counters pretty intimidating, and this can result in impulse buying. If this resonates with you, here are a few things you can do to curb your spending.

1. Doing your homework before you shop goes a long way. Go online and read real reviews and ask friends when you see them wearing something you like.

2. Approach cosmetic counters with confidence. Don't be that girl who looks desperate to drop some dollar, if you don't want to.

3. Ask for samples. Try the product for a week to see if you really like and/or need it.

For more ideas on makeup application, check out YouTube for how-to's. There are loads of online tutorials, which make it easy to follow in real time—you can pause when necessary. Try one of these:

1. **Makeup By TiffanyD.** Clear and easy makeup tutorials on a variety of techniques. Find Tiffany at **www.youtube.com/user/ MakeupByTiffanyD**

2. **Panacea81 (Lauren Luke).** Excellent step-by-step makeup applications. Lauren was the lucky lady from Newcastle, UK whose videos went viral, and with over 60 million views, her YouTube popularity resulted in the creation of her own cosmetic line which is now in Sephora stores all over the US and Canada! Find her at **www.youtube.com/user/panacea81**.

3. **MakeupGeekTV.** Detailed and easy tutorials - **http://www. youtube.com/user/MakeupGeekTV**

Covering Up Dark Circles

If you wake up with dark circles that need brightening up, mix your regular concealer with liquid highlighter and apply it underneath your eyes on your trouble spots. While the concealer covers up the discoloration, the highlighter will reflect any light and reduce the appearance of "bags."

A peachy-colored concealer will counteract the blueness under eyes. This differs from concealing the reddish areas on your face in which you would use a concealer with a greenish hue.

See page 86 for more advice on how to get rid - and avoid- permanent dark circles.

Removing Makeup

Taking makeup off can be extremely damaging to the skin, particularly the super thin skin around the eye. While it might be tempting to pull and drag the skin any which way, this is a sure fire way to encourage wrinkles.

The best way to remove makeup is to use a pre-wet makeup remover pad (adding more water if necessary), and pressing it on the eyelid for 10 seconds. Then, very gently, sweep it across the eyelid, over the eyelashes, and VERY gently under the eye. If there is still some makeup remaining, repeat the process again.

After washing your face, it is always better to pat with a towel rather than rub. Basically, you want to avoid any sort of dragging and pulling of the skin to reduce damage in this area.

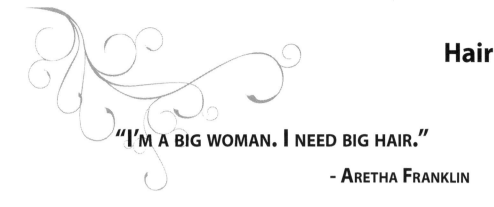

Hair

"I'M A BIG WOMAN. I NEED BIG HAIR."

- **ARETHA FRANKLIN**

Shiny Hair Begins From The Roots!

If you were to visit a hair salon in most Asian countries, a head massage would be included with your cut and blow dry at no extra cost. This is one of the things I miss most about living in Japan! It might also explain why Asian hair is so lustrous and healthy looking- the importance of a healthy scalp for gorgeous hair is certainly something we neglect in the west.

In India, head massage is learned at a young age and is practiced among family members in the home. It is believed to bring benefits, such as promoting hair growth by improving circulation, bringing oxygen and nutrients to the scalp, curing headaches, promoting health and reducing stress and tension. It is even thought to slow down the aging process!

Now, if your fiancé is not up for taking a head massage class or getting his hands all oily, it's time to try some DIY scalp massage. Done over time, hair will become noticeably thicker and healthier as you encourage new hair growth and blood circulation.

How to Perform a Head, Scalp, and Neck Massage

Using oil such as coconut oil, a dedicated Indian massage oil, or even olive oil, massaging your scalp can benefit your entire health, and make you feel calm and relaxed.

> TIP: *When possible, perform the massage directly on the skin and not through clothing. Because excess rubbing can cause irritation, using massage oil is always a good idea. It can get quite messy though, so in situations where it is not possible to use oil, reduce the massage time.*

Start with the Shoulders

Place your right hand on your left shoulder and using your fingers and palm, squeeze any tight spots you can feel. Do this for as long as you like, gradually working up toward the neck. Repeat this with your left hand, working on the right shoulder and up to the right side of the neck. Turn your neck gently and slowly from side-to-side two times, holding for a couple of seconds in each position.

Eyebrows

Take your thumb and first finger and start from between your eyebrows and pinch along each eyebrow. When you reach the temples, gently use your fingertips to massage in circular motions.

Ears

Next, use your fingers to release the tension from your ears. Starting at the ear lobes, pinch a few points working upwards to the top of the ear. Gently press the flap of the ear against your head and hold for a few seconds. (Be careful to avoid touching your eardrum in any way—you should not go near it or let the oil make contact with the inside of the ear.)

Scalp

Take your thumb and fingers up to your hairline and massage in little circles. Gradually work your way up to the crown of the head, continuing to use tiny circles and as much or little pressure as you feel comfortable with. Once you have reached the crown, work back down to the hairline, repeating as many times as you wish.

Finish by taking your fingers to the back of your head and pressing various points gently and slowly. Extend these tiny presses to the back of the neck, taking as long as you like, breathe slowly and relax.

> *If you don't have time to perform a massage but still want to enjoy the benefits oil can offer your hair, you can immerse your hair in oil, tie it back loosely, and sleep this way. When you wash it out in the morning the results should be noticeable - softer and shinier!*

> *Another favorite trick of mine is to heat a wet towel in the microwave and then wrap the towel around the hair coated with oil. (Coconut oil, jojoba oil, olive oil and castor oil are all good options.)*

> *Leave the towel on for 30 minutes and hair will be silky soft after rinsing out and drying. Please do NOT microwave a dry towel! This is a recipe for disaster!*

Whether hair is dry, oily, or normal is genetically fixed, much like our skin. The hair's condition is a result of the follicle's size and shape. As skin care differs for each skin type, so should your hair regime.

Dry Hair

Dry skin is a result of having 20% fewer oil glands to cover the head's surface area compared to that of regular hair. This leads to thirsty, dry hair, which leads to frizz. Dry hair is often wavy or curly, so the frizz can be worsened. You should aim to wash dry hair less than usual—2-3 times a week. Use a conditioner with nut or nut oils in the ingredients - this will add moisture, seal the cuticle and thus minimize frizz. Oh, and be sure to avoid silicone-based shampoos, which also dry out the hair.

Oily Hair

Use a clarifying shampoo once a week and use conditioner only on the tips of the hair, if at all.

Other tips to improve the quality of your hair over the four weeks ahead:

Washing

* The ends of the hair attract the most dirt and build up—clean them thoroughly.

* Rinse out shampoo thoroughly for maximum shine. Shampoo residue results in dull hair.

* Lather for 2-3 minutes with plenty of water.

* Before using a conditioner, squeeze the excess water from your hair. The extra water prevents absorption of the conditioner.

* Avoid washing your hair everyday when possible.

* Wash your hair with warm water rather than hot, and use a low pressure. Hair might be "dead" but it is fragile!

* Unless your hair is very oily, wash the day before the wedding so that your style will hold for longer.

Drying

* When you finish blow-drying, try using the "cool shot" setting on your dryer. Hot air opens the hair cuticle, while cold air closes it, reducing frizz and enhancing shine. For the same reason, rinse your hair with the coldest water you can stand.

* Reduce your usage of hair styling tools as much as possible. I know, I know, I love, LOVE my straighteners too. But going heat-free will dramatically improve the condition of your hair over these 4 weeks.

* If you do use straightening irons, leave 5-10 minutes between blow drying and straightening to let the hair cool down and always use a heat protecting cream or spray! (see below)

* Blot hair with a towel but do not rub.

* Hold the drier 3 inches away from your hair.

Products

* Avoid hair products that contain the following alcohols—Menthanol, Ethanol, Propanol and Isopropyl Alcohol as these will dry out hair. See page 80

* Use a thermal leave-in spray or serum if you use styling tools—this protects hair from heat damage and adds shine. The following are my recommendations, depending on your budget:

$ - Tresemme Thermal Creations Heat Tame Spray, Drug stores.

$$ - Redken Smooth Down Heat Glide Serum, Redken hair salons nationwide.

$$$ - It's a 10 Miracle Leave in Product, Target & drug stores.

* Too much hairspray can weigh down the hair and give it a dull finish.

* Avoid the ingredient Sodium Lauryl Sulphate (SLS). It strips hair of natural oils and can cause a dry, flaky scalp resulting in dandruff. (The reason SLS is in shampoos at all? To create more foam (which people like), and because it's super cheap so it cuts

65

down production costs. SLS isn't necessary, and it will ruin the quality of your hair. Always check the label of your shampoo and skin care products to avoid it!)

Dandruff, Dry Scalp, Seborrhea

You know the deal—white flakes of dead skin on your hair and shoulders and clothes. But did you know that there are actually three types of what is commonly known as "dandruff?"

1. **Dry Scalp**—This is most common in those with dry skin, but can be exasperated by over-processing, too much heat (from sun or your hair dryer), and harsh products. Dry scalp is recognizable as the flakes are small and dry.

   ✱ **Solution:** Use a clarifying shampoo to rid yourself of shampoo residue, which is a major cause of dry scalp. Use an oil treatment that specifies "for dry hair and scalp." Stay away from heat, and improve your diet by increasing your levels of zinc, vitamin B, and Omega 3 oils. (See the section on pages 118 and 119 for recommendations of where to get these nutrients.)

2. **Dandruff**—Dandruff occurs in those with oily scalps and it is the result of a yeast overgrowth, which thrives on excess oil. Hence, the flakes are larger and greasier.

   ✱ **Solution:** Use a tea-tree oil shampoo. Avoid using an anti-dandruff shampoo, which makes your hair dry and while they will mask the problem temporarily, they won't get rid of the cause. The tea-tree oil in shampoo is a natural anti-bacterial and will help fight the growth of yeast. Also limit the frequency with which you wash your hair—it seems counterintuitive, but doing so will reduce the amount of oil you produce and thus curb yeast-growth.

3. **Seborrhea**—This is a more serious scalp condition and is coupled with a red, irritated scalp. Flakes are large and greasy.

* **Solution**: See a dermatologist or your MD. This condition may require prescriptive treatment.

Miscellaneous

* Avoid a radical change of hairstyle before the wedding. There is nothing worse than hating your hair.

* Don't skimp on your hair cuts/coloring. There is a big difference between a $20 cut and a $100 cut, and you should really stretch as far as your purse strings allow to avoid disasters. You'll end up paying for another cut, which will add up in the end.

* Wear a hat in the sun! Sun damages the hair much like it does to the skin.

* Change the position of your elastic hairbands (i.e. switch up low ponytails with high and medium ones) to avoid damage to one area .

* If your hair is dull, your diet might be lacking in vitamin B or Omega oils. Try eating flaxseed, vitamin C and E and fish oils, or taking a supplement. Avocado is also a great hair food!

* Use less shampoo (it can go further than you think), and remember to rinse your hair for about 3-4 minutes. Any less than this and you will be left with an ugly residue—and residual shampoo is a major cause of dull looking hair.

Frizzy Concerns

If frizz is really causing you some concern, consider splashing out on one of these really hair-changing systems. (Note: availability may be limited across the country; check online to see for services near you).

67

The **Japanese Straightening System** *(aka Japanese straight perm)* *uses a combination of chemicals and flat-irons that will keep your hair straight and frizz-free for up to six months. It is also said to look much healthier and shinier. The procedure is getting cheaper as it becomes more widely available, but prices still range from $300-$500. Check online to find a salon that can perform the procedure in your area.*

Brazilian Keratin Treatment *(BKT)—Brazilian blow-outs differ from the Japanese straightening treatment in two major ways. Firstly, it doesn't make hair "poker" straight, rather hair can be wavy, curly and so on, but frizz is eliminated. The second difference is that it is not a chemical treatment, so it is heaps better for your hair, especially if your hair is already damaged. In fact, BKT is designed for damaged hair, turning it from dry and brittle into smooth, less-processed and well-moisturized. You'll be blown away! (Sorry, bad joke).*

The drawback of BKT vs. the Japanese straight perm is that it doesn't last as long, (approximately 3 months vs. 6) even though it is in the same price range.

Locate a salon and find out more at **www.braziliankeratin. com**.

Rain

Although my skin doesn't like California's dry climate, my hair loves it. Never before have I been so frizz-free. However when I go back to England I'm always knocked back into reality. All it takes is a drop of rain and I'm Carrie Bradshaw all over again. Hello 1985!

If there is rain or high humidity on your day, try these tips to minimize frizz:

✽ Don't fight your texture, work with it. Accepting this will be much less painful than trying to win a losing battle, and trust me I know! Don't even try to straighten wavy hair on a rainy day, just let it do it's thing.

✽ Wax helps to reduce frizz - but use it sparingly.

✽ Bobby pins help to put frizzy fly-aways back in their place.

✽ Try to play with your hair as little as possible, despite the temptation to 'touch' it into place. Touching hair just creates more frizz.

✽ Apply anti-frizz serum to sopping wet hair to help control it.

✽ Boar-bristle brushes help control frizz more than plastic bristles—they help the outer layer of the hair to lie flat (which makes hair look shiny) as well as evenly distributing the hair's natural oils from the root to the tip.

✽ Be sure to use a heat-protective spray any time you are using heated appliances. Hair-dryers and straighteners will lead to cuticle damage, leading to frizz. Do your hair a favor and use some protection!

Alcohol in Hair Products— The Good, The Bad & The Ugly

While the general advice is to stay away from alcohol in hair products because it can be incredibly drying, there are in fact a whole host of different alcohols, and some are actually good and condition our hair!

Good Alcohols

Cetyl Alcohol, Stearyl Alcohol, Cetyl Alcohol, Lanolin Alcohol, Lauryl Alcohol, Acetyl Alcohol, Sterol Alcohol

Bad Alcohols

Menthanol, Ethanol, Propanol, Isopropyl Alcohol

Regime For 30 Days

- **Coloring** *(if necessary) 2 weeks before the wedding. Highlights will give flat, limp hair texture.*

- **Shine treatments**—*available at a salon near you.*

- **Hair mask/hot oil treatments.** *These needn't be expensive—you can find them in the drugstore for a dollar or two. Use weekly, particularly if your hair is fine or color-treated, and you will really notice a difference in the condition of your hair.*

- **Avoid heating tools** *as much as possible. Use a thermal spray/serum when using them to reduce damage.*

- *Give yourself a* **head massage** *once a week to encourage hair growth and shine.*

Hands and Nails

"HOLD A TRUE FRIEND WITH BOTH HANDS."

AFRICAN PROVERB

Nails are an excellent indication of our health. They can show signs of nutritional deficiency long before we notice the effects/symptoms elsewhere. Apparently, your hands are the second thing people notice about you after your face. Time to tidy them up!

Hand Care Tips

On the big day get used to your hands being looked at much more than usual. Every lady in sight will want to get a look at your ring and you will probably have some up close and personal ring shots snapped by your photographer.

Because hand skin is very thin and fragile, it can easily dry out or chap. The aging process is also accelerated on this thin skin. Therefore, taking preventative measures to protect hands from the damaging effects of sun, the environment, water, and chemicals is the best way to keep hand skin soft and beautiful.

Get into the habit of wearing gloves when washing up or cleaning since the chemicals in washing cleaning products are very harsh and damaging. You would not wash your face with dish detergent, so don't wash your hands with it! Try to wear gloves in the cold too, and moisturize regularly.

I love the 'paws and claws' (mani/pedi) culture here in the States. It seems that on every street there is a salon offering inexpensive services and with no appointment necessary. Take advantage of it - it's a wonderfully inexpensive luxury! If, however, you are short on time or money, an at-home manicure can easily be done. You can easily perform one the day or night before your wedding.

Manicure

1. Remove all old polish. Use a non-acetone remover on natural nails. (Acetone can cause skin irritation, as well as dizziness and skin problems.)

2. Cut nails into a shape you like—square, round or square with round edges. Use a regular emery board—metal ones will do your nails no good whatsoever. File in one direction. Never use a nail file in a swing motion (it encourages breakages), rather use the whole length and work slowly.

3. Soak hands in warm, soapy water. This helps to soften the cuticles. Alternatively, massage a light cuticle oil into your nails and cuticles.

4. Using a wooden stick, push back your cuticles. I recommend not cutting the cuticles (even though many salons still do this because it looks neat) as it increases the chance of infection.

5. Apply hand lotion.

6. Wipe down nails to ensure a dry surface to apply polish to.

7. Apply base coat.

What is Base Coat?

Base coat is a clear coat that doubles up as a top/finishing coat. It protects the nail from the staining/discoloration that occurs from colored polish. Some brands also offer ingredients such as vitamin E and proteins to moisturize and strengthen the nail. As well as protecting your nail, base coat can help lengthen the life of your manicure.

Try: OPI Natural Nail Base Coat ($8), Sally Hansen Ultimate Shield Fortifying Base & Top Coat ($5).

8. With your desired color, apply the first coat of color from the cuticle to the tip. Start at the side of the nail and cover using several strokes of the brush. Wipe the brush on the side of the bottle before application to avoid having too much polish on your brush, but enough to cover the nail nicely.

9. Wait 2-3 minutes before applying the second coat.

10. Finish with a quick-drying top-coat (clear), which will help the nail to shine and help even out the look.

   Tip: Try not to wear nail varnish continuously; give your nails a breather some weeks. In between manicures make sure to give your nails a good buff. Buffers are cheap, easily available, and renew nails and prevent them from staining yellow.

For Nail Biters

I have friends who have been trying not to bite their nails for several years and I do know it can be a real struggle to quit this habit. One friend of mine can grow her nails really successfully for a few weeks, and then something stressful will happen to trigger her back to bad nail-biting habits.

73

Like a lot of bad habits, there seems to be a lot of psychology behind why people continue to bite their nails despite desperate efforts not to. In situations of nervousness, stress, anxiety and boredom, the habit takes over subconsciously or uncontrollably and all the hard work and will- power becomes undone.

The wedding is one of those occasions where you will be keen to grow out bitten nails. Princess Diana famously clenched her fist when photographers snapped her engagement ring, because of her chewed nails, and while that is always an option, there must be a better way!

Here are some of the methods and products out there designed to help you grow your dream set of nails.

1. Figure out the times/ situations when you decide to start biting- underlying causes of stress, nerves or boredom. Try to deal with these situations in a different way such as taking a walk, going running or writing down what is bothering you.

2. Pick a day to quit. Write it in your schedule and prepare for it – you are going to need distractions, motivation and will-power. Tell people about your challenge and ask them to check up on you.

3. Keep hand cream with you at all times.

4. Keep gloves with you and put them on if you feel the need to bite.

5. Keep your hands busy -with a stress ball, elastic band or something else to play with.

6. Carry chewing gum to keep your mouth busy.

7. Carry a clipper and nail file everywhere. When nails or cuticles snag, cut or file them to resist the urge to chew!

8. To encourage nail growth and to make them harder to bite, use a nail strengthener to help grow your nails. *Try Sally Hansen Growth Miracle* ($8) or *Nail Envy by OPI* ($10)

9. If none of the above work, try anti-biting products which work by making your nails taste foul. Apply it several times a day. *Jessica 'Nibble No More,'* is a no-nail-biting polish with bitter cactus extract to make it taste unappealing ($5 at jessicacosmetics.com). Similar products may be available at your local drug store.

10. Treat yourself to manicures! This will not only encourage you to grow your nails in order to look nice for when you visit the salon, but you will be less inclined to bite them when they are polished and pretty.

Lastly… Be easy on yourself since quitting any bad habit is never going to be easy. Much like anything worth doing, growing your nails requires patience and hard work but also self-reward and encouragement! If you have a set back, start again. Visualize how you want your hands to look, and you'll be half way there. Studies have shown that holding yourself accountable is the best way to break a bad habit, so whether this is keeping a diary of your progress or getting a friend to bug you, make sure to monitor your efforts. Good luck!

If you have weak nails…

* You might be missing something in your diet. Try consuming dairy foods and essential fatty acids (omega 3 is available in oily fish and some fortified milk and eggs.)

* Also be sure that you are getting enough of the Vitamins C, D, E, and B-12 & A in green, yellow and orange veggies.

* Take a multi vitamin as your "insurance policy" to any nutrients missing in your diet.

Other...

* Do not keep your nails colored all the time—give them a breather. Buff nails in between manicures.

* Treat yourself to regular manicures. If you are going to a professional, don't allow the nail technician to trim cuticles too much or too often—there is a risk of bacterial infection and it is unnecessary. Instead ask her to push back the cuticles with a wooden stick.

30 Day Regime

Moisturize often (especially after washing your hands) and keep hand cream in the places that you visit often—the bathroom, kitchen, car, your desk to remind yourself to use it.

Arms—exfoliate with a good body scrub to look beautiful in that dress.

Elbows! (I know right? Never given them a second thought? Well, my little sister used to call this skin "elephant skin." Gross huh? If you want to avoid having elephant skin creep into your cake-cutting pictures, moisturize these too.)

*Make a conscious effort to **quit biting your nails** if you are in the habit of doing so.*

Feet

> ## "I STILL HAVE MY FEET ON THE GROUND,
> ## I JUST WEAR BETTER SHOES."
>
> ### OPRAH WINFREY

Our feet really get the short straw being down there, tucked away in socks, squeezed up in sandals, or held at unnatural heights in our favorite hurt-me-but-cute heels. Morning 'til night, we use and abuse our feet and they really get very little in return. Well, perhaps it's time to show them a little bit of appreciation.

Most people's feet need maintenance! If you are one of those people blessed with baby soft feet, good for you, I am jealous!

Pedicure

At some podiatrist and foot spas, it used to be normal to use razors on the feet to get rid of hard, dry feet. This has since died out due to hygiene concerns (thank goodness), but the same instruments are still available in drug stores and used in the home. These instruments are yet another example of short-term results that in the long term wind up making feet look much worse and can do permanent damage. Once the dry skin is shaved off, the foot doesn't fight back by growing baby soft skin as you might imagine, but hard, defensive, mean skin grows back after a couple of weeks, thus making the problem worse and worse over time.

Please avoid using razor blades to rid the feet of dry skin—the short-term effects might look great, but the long-term effects can be really damaging!

A pumice stone is a much less harsh, natural way of ridding dead skin and allowing new skin to be exposed.

77

Praise for the PedEgg

The ultimate foot file, once only available on As Seen on TV, is now available at regular stores such as Target, drugstores, and online at **www.pedegg.com**.

Reviews of the Ped Egg are very good—ergonomically it is easy to use, creates much less mess than your regular foot file (skin shavings are collected into the egg), and fits into the palm of your hand. The results are also supposed to be very good, especially for removing callouses and very dry, hard skin.

The system is generally quite noninvasive and gentle, but as with all foot files, don't overdo it as this can lead to further skin problems. The website states that those with poor circulation or diabetes should also avoid using the Ped Egg.

At-home Pedicure

Here is a simple pedicure to follow for at-home pedicures

1. While your feet are still dry, use a pumice stone or a specially designed foot file to get rid of the dry skin on your feet. Pay particular attention to the heels and ball of the foot, especially just below the toes.

2. Using an exfoliating gel, wash and scrub your feet in warm water. This can be done in the shower or in a footbath.

3. Cut your nails and push back your cuticles with a wooden stick while they are still soft. Buff nails to create an even texture, and apply polish following the steps from the manicure in the previous section.

4. Apply a lotion to the feet and toenails (peppermint lotion or shea butter.)

5. Wear cotton socks to lock in moisture.

Athlete's Foot (Tinea)

If you are experiencing more than just dry skin, as well as scaling, flaking, itchiness, it might be possible that you have athlete's foot or another bacterial infection.

Having athlete's feet is not a result of dirtiness or not washing your feet, rather it occurs when you don't dry your feet properly, or catch it from a friend or family member who you've shared a shower/towel/sandals with.

– Dry your feet carefully after showering, and use an over-the-counter powder, cream, or spray twice a day for 4-6 weeks. Even after the symptoms have disappeared, continue using for another month and take conscious preventative measures such as keeping your feet dry.

– Wear cotton socks and not nylon.

– Use talcum powder—it dries up moisture and kills infection.

– If persistent or severe, you may need to see a doctor and antibiotics might be required.

– Keeping feet dry is essential to preventing re-infection. Dry between toes thoroughly, wear clean socks, open-toed sandals, and cotton not nylon socks.

– Athlete's foot is highly contagious so make sure to take special precautions to avoid passing it on to anyone that you might share a shower or towel with.

30 Day Regime

Give yourself a *pedicure, or visit the salon for one.*

Get rid of *any infections.*

Deal with dry skin *with regular moisturizing.*

80

Eyelashes and Eyebrows

"WHEN I DIE, THEY'LL PROBABLY AUCTION OFF MY FALSE EYELASHES."

BETTE DAVIS

They say that the eyes are the mirror of the soul. At least, a Yiddish proverb does. We can be deceived by them, persuaded by them, excited by them, lost in them. They say more than words ever can. Of course you want your eyes to look bright and gorgeous on your wedding day as well as any other day.

Let's look at some ways to enhance what your Momma gave you. Open them up with some irresistible faux eyelashes!

Top 3 Faux Eyelashes on the Market

Shu Uemura—*$12-$25 for a set—regarded as the top quality on the market. Glue is purchased separately.*

Mac—*$10-$15—comes in various sizes, shapes, and thickness to suit you. Glue $7 separate.*

Ardell—*$3-$10—a cheaper but good quality option.*

Faux eyelashes can do ridiculously extraordinary things to your look. Suddenly, the amount of makeup you need is drastically reduced as the attention focuses on your eyes, and a big nose or less-than perfect skin no longer hog the limelight!

If your eyelashes are already of quite some length, fake eyelashes may look too "dramatic" on you. Opt for a good eyelash curler and mascara instead.

How to Apply Faux Eyelashes

1. Curl your natural lashes with a pair of eyelash curlers. This will create a nice shape on which to apply the eyelashes. Since it is very difficult to get the false eyelashes exactly on the lashline, using eyeliner close to the eye will allow a little room for error without being noticeable.

2. Apply a blob of special eyelash-adhesive to the back of your hand (left if you are right-handed, right if you are left-handed), and using a pair of tweezers, place the end of the faux eyelash onto the glue. If you are using individual lashes, start from the outer corner of the eye with the longer length ones. Place the lash onto the eyelid. Eyelashes should get shorter as you work toward the inner corner of the eye.

3. If you are using eyelashes on a strip, place the band of the strip onto the eyelid, starting at the inner corner.

4. You can then trim off any excess from the end, and use an eye pencil to disguise any unnaturalness at the eyelid. Never cut the strip at the inner corner—you want shorter lashes here to make it look more natural. You can also trim some length off the individual eyelashes if they are looking undesirably long. Be sure to use the correct strip for each eye—they should be labeled for your left or right eye. Applying the lashes on the wrong eye will make it look less natural as the length of the lashes will be wrong.

TIP—*If using strip eyelashes, place a little more glue on the edges of the lashes than on the rest of them. This is where they will start peeling off first.*

An excellent online tutorial of how to apply eyelashes (and help you feel more confident about it!) can be found here: **http://bit.ly/a11aEA**. (**http://www.youtube.com/user/MakeupGeekTV**)

Eyelash Boosting Products

While faux eyelashes are a great invention, there is no denying that having our own long, full natural lashes would be better than battling with the falsies. So what is the deal with the lash-boosting products available to us these days? Here is a lowdown of your options:

Latisse—$$$

Originally designed as a treatment for the eye condition glaucoma, patients reported longer lashes as a side effect and thus Latisse began to market a gentler version of the prescriptive-strength drug available for sale in stores. **http://www.latisse.com/**

(Please be sure to research potential side effects thoroughly before purchasing.)

Lancôme Precious Cells—$$

Precious Cells mascara claims to strengthen and thicken lashes with ingredients that nourish and condition each lash. It is a mascara and conditioner in one, and it's easy to apply and won't add an extra step to your existing routine if you already wear mascara on a daily basis. Find it at Nordstrom.

L'Oréal's Renewal Lash Serum—$

Worn under mascara and over night, L'Oréal claims that this lash-boosting serum can increase lash length and thickness by up to 25% with no side effects. After completely removing makeup and washing your face, use the bristle-less wand to coat your eyelashes in the serum, and then as you would with an eyeliner, draw a line across the top of your eyelid. You can apply mascara on top so no need to forego your existing makeup routine. Available in drugstores.

Extra-Virgin Olive Oil—$

The bottom line is that these lash-boosting products essentially work by conditioning your lashes and thus reducing hair loss and breakage. For an at-home eyelash boost, coat your eyelashes with olive oil (using a q-tip for easy application) and notice the difference after a week or two.

How long will these results last?

The results should last for around 3-5 months. Think of it like hair dye—new eyelashes will grow back to your original length and thickness in the next cycle of growth.

Mascara

When wearing mascara, try using a primer or conditioner to moisturize the eyelashes before applying it. This can help mascara to last longer and add volume. The primer can be bought separately, or many brands offer a 2-in-1 or 2-step package (a wand with two ends).

When applying mascara, start at the base of the lash, shimmy the wand from left to right, and extend slowly upwards. Pay special attention to the tips of the outer lashes. This will make eyes appear longer and more oval-shaped.

TIP: *Never pump the wand in and out of the tube. This is sometimes done to create a more even application of mascara on the wand, but will dry out your mascara by letting air into the wand, thus drastically shortening it's lifespan.*

Eye Puffiness/Bags

Eye puffiness can be caused by stress, fluid retention, allergies, a lack of sleep, or too much salt.

Talk to your doctor about antihistamines if you think the puffiness is a result of allergies. If sleeping more and cutting down on salt is not working for you, try an eye cream with antioxidants and vitamin K. Also look for the ingredients coffee berry or green tea.

Steeped teabags once a week also help to relieve puffiness. Take two green tea bags and place them in hot water to remove some of the tea and encourage the tannins to come out. Put them in the fridge to cool, and once cooled, place on top of each eye for 10-15 minutes. You can also try applying slices of cucumber, a spoon from the freezer, or ice cubes for three-to-five minutes, just as you would if you had swelling in any other part of the body.

Top 3 Ways to Avoid Eye Puffiness

1. *Steeped teabags or sliced cucumber for 5-10 minutes at a time.*

2. *Sleep—sleep more and with more than one pillow (this encourages drainage of toxins).*

3. *Reduce salt and alcohol and drink more water—8-10 glasses a day.*

For dark circles rather than puffiness, try a specially-formulated eye cream. *Tricia Sawyer Eye Slept* (**www.triciasawyer.com**) is a great dark circle busting treatment ($21).

> TIP—*The potassium in raw potato slices can bleach away darkness too—use them in the same way you would use sliced cucumbers.*

Eyebrows and Face Shape

It is amazing how bad we are at judging our own symmetry in the mirror. There is, in my opinion, nothing worse than sitting across the table from someone and being completely distracted by the fact that they have one eyebrow that is longer than the other, or there is complete dissymmetry between the two. I can't stand it! I am inclined to stare at them, and I'm not even realizing I'm doing it. (This is something that used to get me in trouble with my high school Math teacher; I was completely obsessed by the fact that her teeth were unbelievable wonky. I was fascinated by the mixed-up terrain they had taken on, and couldn't help but focus on them when I was answering questions in class. At least in terms of maintaining eye contact with somebody, the eyebrows are located conveniently close to the eyes…)!

It is wise to see a professional to shape your eyebrows at least once, and then you can follow the shape by plucking any new hairs as they grow back. Those of us who haven't always gone the professional route have probably had more than their fair share of eyebrow disasters. I've been there - done that- too many times. Now I head to the Benefit Eyebrow Bar, found in many department and Benefit stores across the country, once in a blue moon and then maintain the stray hairs in between visits. You can get a wax and shape for roughly $20 (plus tip).

There are generally six types of face shapes. The shape of your eyebrows should fit the shape of your face.

Which shape are you? (If you're not sure, get a second opinion from a friend. It's hard to judge yourself).

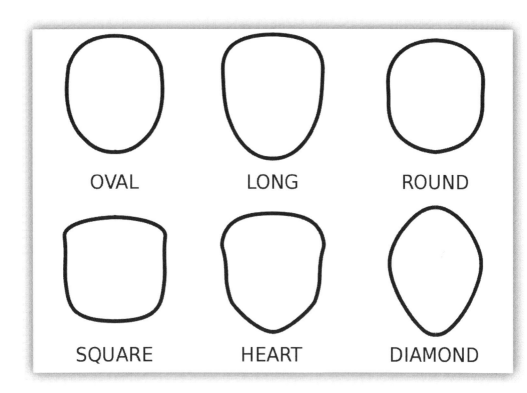

1. Oval—a soft angled brow shape will work best.

2. Long—flat brows will help your face appear shorter.

3. Round—high-arched brows will make your face look longer.

4. Square—thicker, stronger brows will balance a heavier jaw line.

5. Heart—rounded brows are the most flattering for a heart-shaped face.

6. Diamond—curves will soften your look and make the widest portion of your face look less wide.

Eyebrow Pencil Color/Powder

The general rule when choosing an eyebrow pencil color or powder is to go a shade darker than your natural brow color.

* Blondes—use a light brown.

* Redheads—try honey-colored.

* Brunettes—go with a deep brown color.

After filling in your shape with pencil or eye shadow, use a clear brow gel to hold brows in place. Vaseline also works well for this purpose.

How to Shape Your Eyebrows Successfully

To create the perfect arch shape, hold a pencil vertical to your nose bridge. This is where the eyebrow should start. Then hold the pencil diagonally, from the corner of your nose across the iris. The peak of the arch should be where the pencil hits the eyebrow. Finally, slant the pencil so that it goes from the corner of your nose, past the outer corner of your eye and hits your brow. This is where your brow should finish.

TIP—*For smaller eyes, make your brows a little thicker, and for close-together eyes, widen the space in-between the brows. This will create a visual illusion.*

* Don't pluck the hair above your eyes -it will grow back messy and awkward.

* Pluck individual hairs at a time, one hair can make a big difference!

* Stand back from mirror periodically. Do not use a magnifying mirror when plucking your eyebrows! This will totally throw your sense of perspective.

* Hold the skin around your brow taut to ease the pain.

* Pluck after a warm shower as the pores are slightly open and this will minimize the pain.

* If you make a mistake and over pluck, use an eye pencil (or eyebrow powder/eye shadow for a more natural finish) to "fill in the gaps."

Threading is a more accurate alternative to waxing and can be found in malls and in salons across the country.

30 Day Regime

*Try an **eyelash-boosting product** if you desire.*

Practice applying fake eyelashes if you wish to use them on your wedding day.

*Get eyebrows **professionally shaped** or do it yourself.*

Get rid of undereye puffiness and circles.

Hair Removal

My first wax "down there" was anything but pleasant. I went first, but my best friend backed out as she witnessed my muffled screams and the expression on my face. Geez, thanks! Who would have known that we put ourselves through such misery. I'm fidgeting in my chair just thinking about it. Oh gawd!

I suppose the good news is that waxing does get less painful the more often you partake. The second piece of good news is that there are several (arguably less painful) alternatives available. It might take some uncomfortable experimentation, but if you dream of being hair-free and care-free, it'll be worth the somewhat awkward journey.

Here are the most popular options for body and facial hair removal:

1. Shaving—The least painful, cheapest, and easiest way to remove leg and underarm hair and one we are all probably familiar with. If shaving the underarm area, be sure to maneuver the razor from side to side as well as up and down—hair here is particularly thick and grows in different directions.

<u>Good For:</u> Legs, underarm, bikini area when you have little time.

<u>Not So Good For:</u> Those with dark, thick hair may find that shaving is not an adequate solution. Especially those with curly hair, which can grow back painfully, thicker, and far too quickly. Avoid shaving arms and face, it's just a bad idea, period.

2. Waxing—A relatively inexpensive, effective, and long-lasting solution. Warm wax is applied to the hair and a strip is then placed on top and ripped away. Imagine ripping off a very strong Band-Aid—it is the same burning sensation. The hair will be taken with it, leaving behind a smooth, hair-free surface that will last for 3-4 weeks. Hair will also grow back finer, and with time may grow back much slower or not at all.

Good For: Arms, legs, underarm, bikini and facial hair, though it can be very painful, especially the first few times.

Not So Good For: It is also not recommended for those with skin conditions/eczema/sensitive skin.

Locate a salon with a good reputation near you at www.Yelp.com.

3. Sugar waxing/sugaring—Sugaring is highly effective and works very much like waxing. A paste made from sugar, water, lemon juice, and other natural ingredients removes the hair from its root but doesn't adhere to skin, so it is supposedly less painful than waxing. Additionally, the paste is warmed by the body's natural heat so it doesn't need to be boiled beforehand and can't burn your skin. It is slightly more expensive than regular waxing, but if you don't like the pain of waxing it is a great option.

Good For: Legs and arms

4. Depilatory cream—if you ever tried this in the 1990's…thankfully it doesn't smell anything like it used to!

Veet is one brand that offers a reasonably good-smelling product. Nair is also a popular option. Always do a patch test before using on an entire area!

Good For: Arms, legs, bikini

Not So Good For: May cause skin irritation especially on sensitive skin. Don't use on body parts not specified on the box—skin is of different thickness in different areas!

5. Laser Hair Removal—Laser beams are used to heat the hair follicle and destroy any potential of regrowth. Several treatments spread over several months will result in no regrowth, ever!

Pain-wise, laser hair removal has been likened to stinging or pinching, so while it is not a comfortable feeling, it is by no means unbearable.

Side effects may include reddening or swelling, but this typically goes away within a few hours. On rare occasions, some blistering or bruising may occur, but typically resolves quickly. Sun exposure should be limited post-treatment.

<u>Good For:</u> Facial hair, underarms and all over (though the bigger the area the more expensive it costs). Long lasting.

<u>Drawbacks:</u> Very costly; treatments must be spread over a few months.

6. Epilation—Pulls hair out deep at roots, similar to waxing. It is as painful (at least at first) as waxing and tweezing.

<u>Good For:</u> Areas where long-lasting effects are desired—arms, underarms, legs. Be sure to exfoliate well afterwards to avoid in-growing hairs when there is re-growth.

Facial Hair

Take care of facial hair removal (lip, brows, chin) a week before your wedding. This gives post-waxing bumps, redness, and inflammation time to subside. Waxing of facial hair can be done at home or in the salon. Using a depilatory cream is another option. Results will last for one week.

Bleaching can conceal dark hair rather than removing it (for example: above the lip where the skin can be delicate).

The Bikini Wax

If waxing your bikini line, you should allow the hair to grow to 1/4- 1/2 inch length in order for the wax to have something to hold on to. A good professional wax will last for 4-6 weeks, well into the honeymoon!

Okay, so no one is going to see this, except for whichever lucky friend is helping you put on your dress. But having a tidy downstairs will make you feel like a million dollars, I am sure of it.

It will hurt though. The term "No Pain, No Gain" was surely coined with this procedure in mind. Wax is applied to the unwanted hair and ripped away with a strip. Given the nature of the thin, sensitive skin down there, it will be an uncomfortable pain. Here are some tips to minimize the pain as much as possible:

1. Your pain threshold is lowest during your period so avoid any kind of waxing during this time. The week after your period is when your pain threshold is at it's highest.

2. Take a painkiller one to two hours beforehand.

3. Try using an antiseptic topical numbing cream over the targeted area 30-45 minutes ahead of the wax. Examples include Dr Numb Numbing Cream (<u>www.drnumb.com</u>), No Scream Cream (<u>www.relaxnwax.com</u>), and LMX 5 Cream (available at drug stores).

Deciphering the Bikini Wax Menu

The American/ The Natural—*this follows the traditional panty line.*

The French—*goes a little further and leaves a small strip of hair, aka the "landing strip."*

The Brazilian—*everything off! Everything, all the way back there too!*

Please note: sometimes salons create their own names for bikini waxes e.g. the Hollywood, the Traditional and so on. Please ask for clarification, including on the terms above to get exactly what you walked in for!

Any random hairs

You know the kind that just show up uninvited? Tweeze the suckers!

30 Day Regime

*Take care of hair removal ensuring that any procedures that may cause swelling or redness are finished **at least two days prior** to the wedding day.*

Beauty Product Ingredients To Avoid

Recently there has been a shift toward natural ingredients in products in the beauty industry and for good reason. While unnatural chemicals may help keep the cost of products down, nobody knows exactly what the side effects of the ingredients might be, particularly when they are mixed together—known as the "Cocktail Effect." It is best to be proactive when choosing your products and at least check the labels for the following ingredients;

* SLS (Sodium Lauryl Sulphate): penetrates the protective barrier of the skin, damaging its protective function. It also dries out the skin and causes skin irritation, especially in those already suffering from eczema or dermatitis. It is also feared that it contains carcinogenic properties, and when found in toothpaste might be the cause of mouth ulcers.

Found in: soaps, shampoos, detergents and toothpastes.

Confusingly, Sodium **Laureth** Sulphate however, is okay.

* The alcohols: Isopropyl Alcohol, Methanol, and Ethanol listed in the first five ingredients on the label will dry out the skin and cause irritability. (They have also been said to cause nausea, headaches, dizziness, and depression.)

Found in: lotions, fragrances, and several kinds of cosmetics.

* Lacquer—this is often added to waterproof mascara. May thin the lashes and lead to lash loss.

For You, Au Naturale Ladies

While many products might state "natural" or "organic" on their packaging, the regulations are still evolving and may not count for much. However, The Natural Products Association has produced a natural seal given to those products where 95% of the ingredients are truly natural and pose no human health risks.

Burt's Bees is of the widely-available product lines they recommend and contain no SLS or phthalates. To find out more or check out other companies, visit http://www.npainfo.org/, or check out their great buyer's guide at http://naturalproductsbuyersguide. com/.

Cellulite

"If 90 percent of all women have cellulite, then isn't it normal?"

Rona Berg

Sure, it gets worse with weight gain, but even skinny ladies can get cellulite since it is not about being overweight (a common myth) but is generally the result of a build up of toxins in the body. Therefore, the main aim when trying to reduce cellulite is to avoid taking in toxins, and make sure that those already in the body can leave quickly and efficiently. Other than that, it might just be one of those things we have to learn to love about ourselves. No expensive cream is going to work miracles on this one. Here are some things that may help:

Top 10 Things You Can Do To Reduce Cellulite

1. Stick to a low fat diet.

2. Limit tea, coffee, alcohol, cigarettes.

3. Reduce your salt intake.

4. Take a multi-vitamin.

5. Drink lots of water.

6. Avoid processed, unnatural ingredients—these are difficult for the body to digest and results in toxins. Eat organically where possible, and include lots of fruit and vegetables.

7. Eat a diet high in fiber.

8. Move your legs as much as possible—don't sit down for long periods of time without moving.

9. Eat protein with every meal.

10. Dry body-brushing!

Dry Body Brushing—A Great Way To Detoxify

- *The logic behind dry body brushing is that by improving your circulation, the blood will then deliver nutrients and oxygen to the areas where cellulite sits, as well as taking away toxins from these areas. Additionally, dry body brushes get rid of dead skin cells much like exfoliation, improving the skin's appearance.*

- *The texture of a body brush should not be too stiff or scratchy, but bristles that are too soft won't work. Choose natural bristles over synthetic ones, and as its name suggests, use on dry skin. Preferably before getting in the shower (because you will be shedding dead skin), start at your feet and use the brush in long, deep strokes. As a general rule you should be stroking in the direction of the body's core. The main lymph nodes are in the armpits and groin, and this is where toxins can exit the body. Stroking in the direction of them encourages toxins to politely leave through these exit points.*

- *Continue brushing all over the body, including the arms, and pay special attention to the areas that are cellulite prone—usually the thighs and butt. When you first begin dry body brushing, your skin may become quite red. This is a good sign—your circulation is working well, and blood is getting to hard to reach areas. Try to get into a habit of doing this*

before getting in the shower and you will notice a difference in the condition of your skin and any cellulite dimples you have found!

- *Dry body brushing in the morning is best as it boosts your circulation and wakes you up!*

- *Body brushes can be found from health and beauty stores— they are also known as "massage brushes." Try one of these: Earth Therapeutics ($6) from the Drugstore.com, or the Body Shop ($12).*

Stretch Marks

These reddish purple lines that become silvery or white over time are exactly what they claim to be—marks from the stretching of the skin! Whenever you gain or lose weight you may notice them, as well as when "parts" of you experiences rapid growth- they appear most commonly on the stomach, thighs, hips, breasts, upper arms and lower back.

The most important thing to know about stretch marks is that they pose no health risks whatsoever. They are only a nuisance for aesthetic reasons. The silvery-white marks are more noticeable (though not more common), on olive and darker skin.

It used to be said that once you had them they would never go away. Then laser treatment was invented and that became an expensive, yet effective option for removing them. More recently a promising and far less expensive option comes in the shape of a pot of shea butter.

Advice from Africa

The karite tree (also known as the shea tree) grows the nuts which shea oil and butter is made from. The majority of the world's shea butter comes from these trees in Africa, and it is used religiously

there for a plethora of reasons. It is believed to help make hair shine, reduce the effects of the sun and protect against wrinkles. But one of its most effective roles is to reduce the appearance of stretch marks. If it works, what a cheap and easy way to get rid of them— worth a try!

If you are planning to lose or gain weight for whatever reason (e.g. pregnancy), shea or cocoa butter seems to be a wonderful preventative measure against stretch marks.

Part II
Health

"THE GREATEST WEALTH IS HEALTH."

-VIRGIL

*O*f all the things that could happen on your big day, or the weeks leading up to it, you or the groom being sick has to be one of the worst possible scenarios. It was certainly my biggest fear. The best thing you and the hubby-to-be can do is to take care of yourselves no matter how stressed out and crazy busy things get.

Firstly, eat right!

"LET FOOD BE THY MEDICINE AND LET THY MEDICINE BE FOOD."

-HIPPOCRATES

Secondly, taking precautions not to get sick is crucial—wash your hands often, use anti-bacterial gel when you are outside of the house, sleep!, and take your vitamins. None of this is rocket science, but somehow we tend to leave this kind of common sense behind when we graduate from high school.

The aim of this section is to help you feel your best: it includes advice on nutrition and exercise, a "super food" shopping list, as well as a 30-day eating plan to up the fiber levels in your diet if that is something you need. It also covers stomach issues and their possible causes and solutions, how to ensure you dine out in the healthiest way, exercises to help you tone up within 30 days, and advice on how to avoid the cold and flu monsters!

Water

"A MAN OF WISDOM DELIGHTS IN WATER."

- CONFUCIUS

We've all heard it a million times before. Water is GREAT for you, etc etc etc!

In my experience, there are two kinds of people—those whose bodies naturally crave water and don't even have to think twice about drinking it. Their bodies want it and desire it. At restaurants, these people will have their glass of water continuously refilled until the check comes, unaware that they have finished three or four large glasses.

Those in the other camp must make a conscious effort to drink water. Without paying attention, they can go a whole day surviving on coffee, soda, or perhaps no liquid whatsoever! Yes, it is true that we do receive water from our foods, but not a substantial amount and nowhere near enough. If you fall into the latter group, you need an action plan to up your intake.

How about picking up a reusable bottle (a liter is good), and making sure that you refill it at least twice (if not a third time) during the day? Yes, you are going to pee more. If your fear of public bathrooms is the reason why you don't drink water in the first place, get over it. It is much more healthy and normal to be drinking and peeing regularly than avoiding all those germs in the bathroom. If you don't like the taste of water so much, try adding lemon juice. Not only does this taste good, it is also a detoxifying tonic that will add to your vitamin C intake and will help to prevent catching viruses. You could also try flavored water as an alternative to the real deal, but be aware of the high sugar content.

Why Water Is SO Great For You (In case you need reminding!)

Without getting into too much biology, water is essential to ALL of our bodily processes, and thus it will be apparent on the outside whether or not you are drinking enough water. It brings nutrients to each cell and carries away the waste products. It acts as a lubricant for joints and helps the digestive process. It is vital to our body temperature regulation, affects our energy levels, and makes sure that all our organs are properly doing their thing.

7 Reasons Why We Should Be Drinking More Water:

* Detoxification of the skin and kidneys. This will give you that healthy glow.

* Often when we are hungry, we are in fact thirsty. Drinking more water helps to maintain a healthy weight.

* Water is a great appetite suppressant and contains no fat, carbs, calories, or sugar.

* Being dehydrated makes you feel tired and drains you of energy.

* Drinking more water will reduce the number of headaches you get since headaches are a symptom of dehydration.

* Drinking more water can cure constipation.

* If you are in need of losing a few pounds and have a soda/milk/fruit juice habit, by doing nothing other than making water your choice of drink, you could effortlessly lose 10-15 pounds a year!

How Much?

The amount you should be drinking varies per person and depends upon a number of factors. These include your size, health, activity levels, and the climate you live in.

Whilst the '8 glass rule' is often banded about and is a nice aim, this isn't for everyone. A good general rule is to drink enough water so that your urine is colorless or only slightly yellow. You should be peeing around 6-8 times a day if you are getting enough water. (If you are taking Vitamin C supplements or other medications, color may vary. Please check the packet!) Being thirsty means that your need for water has gone too far. You are already dehydrated if you are experiencing fatigue, weakness or dizziness, headaches or irritability. Don't let yourself get to this stage by remembering to sip regularly and often.

Cultural Tidbit

Chinese Medicine and Drinking Water Temperature

The verdict is still out on whether ice, room temperature, or warm water is better for you, but Traditional Chinese Medicine argues that warm water is best for facilitating digestion and keeping the bowels regular. It also states that warm water and/or tea can help to break down the greasy fats in a meal and that is the secret to staying slim.

Try and up you water intake over the next 30 days and notice the difference!

Nutrition

"IF YOU WANT TO BE BEAUTIFUL, YOU NEED TO EAT!"

ME.

Okay it sounds boring, but the best advice when it comes to eating right, is to eat "clean". And I'm not talking about hygiene here. Eating clean means eating as naturally as possible. If a label has a ton of ingredients that you can't pronounce let alone know the meaning of, it is probably not delivering much nutritional value and making our liver, bowels, and kidneys work hard. As a general rule, the shorter the list of ingredients on a food label, the better it is for you. Additionally, when consuming calories we should try to take in calories of value and avoid the empty ones as much as possible.

Empty Calories = High Calories but Low Nutrition

For example, a can of soda and medium-sized banana may both contain 120 calories, but one is empty calories while the other is packed with nutritious value. Those 120 calories could be working for us—our skin, our organs, our brain—or providing us with energy and nothing more. In other words, make sure these calories are working for you! Think *value for your calories.*

Additionally, eating frequently will keep your metabolism boosted and your energy levels high. Don't wait until you're about to pass out; aim for three meals a day plus small sensible snacks mid-morning and afternoon if you start to feel hungry. (See page 133 for healthy snack ideas.)

The Bottom Line

It is not through sheer luck that gorgeous, slim, and healthy women are born that way (though sometimes it might appear so). Most of these women are pro active in making conscious choices, and if needs be, plan ahead accordingly! Our society is becoming overweight and sick with health issues for a reason—there are too many unhealthy options available, and the portion sizes are getting out of control.

Plan Ahead

Be a little strategic with your eating habits; pay attention and force yourself to choose healthy options. Read menus online before going to the restaurant so that you don't make a terrible choice in the face of hunger. Keep your house stocked with fresh, healthy options instead of junk food. In order to stay slim and healthy for life, your mindset should change from viewing healthy eating as a restrictive, boring temporary thing to an exciting and adventurous way of life. Just think of the benefits you will gain—more energy, clearer skin, fewer colds and more confidence to name a few! And the good news is that you don't need to be a stickler to healthy eating! Abiding by these principles 80% of the time will allow you to reap the benefits of healthy eating while not missing out on your favorite foods and treats. So what kinds of food should you aim to include in your diet?

Superfoods!

While nutritionists advocate a wide and varied diet, there are a few "superfoods" that should regularly be on every lady's grocery list! Superfoods are food types that pack a massive nutrient punch per gram, so by eating them you can enjoy a whole range of benefits. Find 12 of them listed below in no particular order.

1. Berries

—Berries are full of antioxidants, higher than the levels in red wine or tea, which reduce free-radical damage and may lower your chances of getting cancer. They are also very high in Vitamin C, which will strengthen your immune system. Vitamin C reduces skin damage and improves the skin's appearance in general.

How To Include Them: Blueberries, blackberries, strawberries, logan berries, cranberries, bilberries, gooseberries...the list goes on. Try adding them to cereal, yogurt, or making smoothies.

2. Nuts

—non-salted is best! All kinds, but especially walnuts.

Walnuts are one of the best plant sources of protein. They are high in fiber, and contain lots of B vitamins as well as Vitamin E. They also contain magnesium and very high amounts of Omega 3 fatty acids, much more so than other nuts. They are also fabulous for heart health.

Many women stay clear of nuts because of their high calorie and fat content. The key, as always, is moderation (stick to 10-20 nuts at a time, not an entire bag), and garner their super health benefits by eating them in place of other high fat, but less nutritious foods.

How To Include Them: Snack on them instead of chips or cookies, toss them into your salads or pasta instead of meat or cheese, add them to your breakfast cereal or pizza—get creative!

3. Whole Grains

The term "whole grain" is thrown around a lot these days. A bit of research tells me that "a grain is considered whole when all three parts—bran, germ and endosperm—are present." In terms of health benefits, whole grains contain a good source of B vitamins, Vitamin E, magnesium, iron and fiber as well as other valuable antioxidants!

Whole grains include brown rice, whole wheat flour, oatmeal, brown bread, barley, bulgar, popcorn, quinoa and many cereals. The US government's dietary guidelines recommend eating three servings a day.

How To Include Them: Replace all white, processed food with the brown version—white bread with brown bread, white rice with brown rice, white flour with brown flour and so on. Many restaurants offer these versions nowadays, too. Again the 80% rule is good here—try eating brown rice and bread at home and having white rice and bread when you eat out if you really miss it.

4. Dark Greens

Dark green vegetables include broccoli, spinach, asparagus, green beans, and also the less popular and slightly more intimidating options such as kale, chard, collard and bok choy. They all contain wrinkle-fighting vitamins A and C, as well as those damn things that many women need but often lack—iron and calcium. They are very filling and high in fiber, but low in calories, which makes it hard not to love them.

How To Include Them: Try boiling and steaming them if you enjoy their natural flavor. If you don't, get adventurous—sauté them with soy sauce, add your favorite low calorie salad dressing, or hide them in pasta or a lasagna.

5. Flaxseed

Flaxseed is another fantastic source of Omega 3 fatty acids, particularly for vegetarians. It is full of cancer-fighting anti-oxidants (most noticeably for breast cancer), is high in fiber, and contains many heart-health benefits. Flaxseed is also high in vitamins and minerals, including iron, potassium, zinc, magnesium, calcium, and phosphorous.

The additional benefits of flaxseed:

For anyone with IBS or digestive disorders, flaxseed feeds the "good" bacteria in the intestines. It is also great for those with acne, memory problems, or poor circulation!

How To Include It: Sprinkle ground flaxseed on your cereal, salads and in yogurt and smoothies. Cook it with rice or bread items (pancakes, muffins etc.) Use it as a healthier alternative to breadcrumbs when breading fish or meat.

Tip: *Many people have asked me where you can get flaxseed, and the good news is that it is becoming more available as it gains attention in the media. Find it in the baking section in regular grocery stores (with the sugar, flour and so on), or sometimes near the nuts, seeds, and dry fruit section. Some supermarkets such as Trader Joe's and Wholefoods offer a variety of flaxseed-based products such as bread, tea and peanut butter, as do natural and organic specialist stores.*

6. Oily Fish, especially Salmon

Oily fish includes salmon, trout, mackerel, sardines, pilchards, herring, kipper, eel, whitebait, and fresh tuna (but not the canned kind).

Oily fish is another great source of protein and Omega 3 fatty acids.

It also

* Reduces levels of bad cholesterol in the blood

* Increases the levels of good cholesterol

* Lowers blood pressure

* Protects the heart

* Is good for the brain

* Is good for the eyes

* Protects from Alzheimer's/dementia

* Reduces the risk of depression

* Is a good source of important minerals.

* Helps the body to fight stress and produce energy.

How To Include It: Substitute fish for meat occasionally. It is recommended that women of child-bearing age eat oily fish once a week, but no more than twice. One portion is 140 grams.

7. Green Tea

Used as a natural medicine in China for 4,000 years, green tea is full of powerful antioxidants (catechins, flavanoids, polyphenols) that fight free radical damage and have the potential to fight cancer and heart disease. Drinking green tea neutralizes the harmful effects of UV rays to the skin. This may help to explain why Japanese women, who tend to drink green tea 2-3 times a day, look so young! Additionally, green tea is a good anti-bacterial for the teeth and mouth, and drinking it three times a day has been shown to increase the metabolism.

How To Include It: Green tea can be consumed hot or cold. Try adding lemon or honey if the taste is too bitter for you. Green tea can be used as a replacement for coffee—the caffeine content is still high, but it is released slowly over time, unlike coffee which tends to give us more of a "hit."

What Are Free Radicals Anyway?

You have probably heard the term "fights free radical damage" on one too many TV commercials. But does anybody know what the these free radicals really are?

The simplified explanation is that free radicals are unstable molecules that naturally occur in the body, and have an unpaired electron. To become stable, they must steal an electron from another molecule around them. The molecule that loses the electron however, then becomes unstable and hence must find another molecule to steal from! This chain reaction leads to premature aging, a lowered immune system, and an increased risk of disease.

Antioxidants are stable molecules which can donate an electron to stabilize the free radical without causing a chain reaction. Thus they help to prevent aging and strengthen the immune system.

8. Dark Chocolate

I know you like this one!

The flavanols (powerful antioxidants) in dark chocolate are thought to improve your skin's condition and leave it softer and less sensitive. In addition, dark chocolate is thought to be a good mood booster and can improve the skin's resistance to UV rays. Unlike milk chocolate, dark chocolate will leave you satisfied after a square or two, while milk chocolate is less satisfying and can be devoured endlessly. Dark chocolate also has less fat and sugar than the milk variety.

How To Include It: Need you ask?

9. Yogurt

It sounds pretty gross, but yogurt is full of active, so-called "good" bacteria. These are also known as probiotics, which means "for life," and it will balance the digestive system. Yogurt is great for those bloated days or for reducing intestinal discomfort of any kind.

Yogurt also has loads of protein and calcium, which is great for bone and teeth health. (Calcium prevents loss of bone density, which is particularly important for young women.)

The good bacteria in yogurt has tons of other benefits too—it discourages vaginal yeast infections, strengthens the immune system, and helps balance levels of bacteria in the gut after taking a course of antibiotics. Just be sure to choose a yogurt that actively claims to contain probiotics, live or active cultures.

How To Include It: Eat it for breakfast, dessert, add it to cereal or fruit and seeds. Cook with it in place of cream or crème fraiche in recipes. (Cooking with yogurt is a low-fat alternative to cream or crème fraiche; however, heating it will destroy the good bacteria/ probiotics.)

10. Tomato

This is that funny veggie that is actually not a vegetable at all but a fruit (you still won't catch me drinking tomato juice for breakfast though. Urgh!)

Its main property lycopene, is a super anti-oxidant that flushes out free-radicals, helping prevent several kinds of cancer. Consuming tomatoes with olive oil or avocado produces optimum absorption into the body.

Tomatoes also contain tons of vitamin A (beta carotene), C and E, as well as the mineral zinc, which are great for skin health.

How To Include It: Slice them up into salads, pastas, on pizzas, or roast them whole and eat with risotto.

11. Eggs

Yes, your Gran (and a few studies) told you that eggs will raise your cholesterol levels and it's true to a certain extent. But the sad thing is that these studies didn't focus on the benefits of eggs of which there are loads!

Eggscellent Source of Cholesterol?

The body makes its own cholesterol for hormones as well as for cell membranes, so often high cholesterol levels are hereditary rather than diet-related. Eggs may raise your cholesterol levels, but as with anything, just don't sit down and eat four at once.

Eggs are a great source of high quality protein, Vitamin K and are low in calories. Additionally, eggs have been touted as being super for eye health.

Eggs are also high in choline—a nutrient that 90% of the US is deficient in, which is really important for brain and nervous system regulation.

How To Include Them: Scrambled, poached, boiled, fried, omelets— good for breakfast, lunch or dinner!

12. Bananas

Bananas are full of potassium, which is good for heart health and blood pressure levels. They are also an excellent source of fiber, and keep you full for a long time due to their makeup of complex carbohydrates. They also contain tryptophan, which helps to release serotonin—a hormone that's responsible for lifting your mood. They are also a superb cure for hangovers!

How To Include Them: As they are, sliced on cereal, or in smoothies. Try blending soy milk, a ripe banana, and a handful of blueberries for a snack or a nutritious breakfast.

TIP: *A great resource to help you analyze your diet can be found at* **http://www.whfoods.com/fdanalyzer.php**. *Answer a few questions about your eating habits and receive the advice of a personal food advisor without the price tag!*

The Organic Debate

Organic Food & Products—Why Choose Them?

The definition of "organic" is something along the lines of "free of chemicals as well as non-natural fertilizers and pesticides." Organic foods, clothing, and supplies are also free from the growth hormones fed to some factory farmed animals, as well as being non-genetically modified. What does this mean exactly?

Studies have found the following in support of organic practices:

* Organic farming uses, on average, 30% less energy that regular farming.

* Depending on the produce, organic food has higher levels of Vitamin C, E, Calcium, Iron and Zinc (up to 40% more).

* Organic milk has an average of 68% more Omega 3 fatty acids than non-organic milk.

* You have a lowered risk of contracting food poisoning by eating organically.

* Organic practices support sustainability and improved environmental conditions. Not using toxic chemicals is better for our land, sea, and wildlife, too.

As well as reducing your exposure to these chemicals and being better for the environment, you won't find artificial sweeteners or preservatives in organic food—a bonus!

115

Organic food can be more expensive than the regular stuff, so it is understandable if purchasing organic does not jibe with your budget. It doesn't have to be all or nothing - you can choose to buy organic food where possible and where you feel it to be important. For example, you might commit to buying organic red meat and milk and nothing else (cows in the US are still being fed with hormones and antibiotics (rBGH), even though this process is banned in the EU and Asia.)

A Note On The Preparation Of Food

Steaming your food preserves more nutrients than boiling or microwaving as the food does not come into direct contact with water; it is the steam that is cooking the food. It is also a delicious way to cook root vegetables such as sweet potatoes, carrots, and yams. Try it!

Vitamins/Minerals Often Lacking in Young Ladies

A Note on Multi-Vitamin Tablets

A few years ago I was complaining to my friend about how I had been feeling a bit run down and that perhaps it was because I hadn't been taking my vitamins regularly. She quizzed me as to why not. I couldn't really give her an answer other than, "Well, I forget. And I don't really enjoy swallowing something the size of a piece of sushi, either." (So I was exaggerating on the size thing.) She totally whooped my butt about this! I guess I was being pretty lazy in neglecting to take one tasteless pill everyday. And besides,

for wusses like me, there are chewy vitamins, which I actually enjoyed taking as a kid. Don't be lazy like I was or else my friend will come and hunt you down.

No matter how well you eat, there are many reasons why you might not be getting all the nutrients you need, and taking a high-quality vitamin will act as your safety blanket (but should not act in place of a varied and sensible diet!). Look for one that is designed for women and for vegetarians /vegans if you follow either of these diets.

Recommended Multi-Vitamin Brands

Since multi-vitamins are not regulated by the FDA, the quality of them varies wildly. Some will give you far too much of the RDA, others won't give you enough. Here are the multi-vitamin brands that actually provide the adequate amounts of the vitamins and minerals you should be consuming each day;

1. *One-A-Day Women's Multivitamin*, $27 for 250 tablets.

2. *Centrum Ultra Women's Multivitamin/Multimineral Supplement*, $20 for 200 tablets.

3. Drugstore brand vitamins often have the same ingredients as those recommended above, but at a fraction of the price. Put your local store's brand to the test by comparing the labels side-to-side and checking that you are getting the same necessary vitamins and minerals, including iron.

    Note for vegetarians: Purely vegetarian multivitamins are harder to find, as most contain gelatin. They do exist but with a higher price tag – try the Pure Encapsulations range at www.purecaps.com.

In the next few pages, I've notated what's important for us young women to include in our diet.

*RDA means Recommended Dietary Allowance or Recommended Daily Allowance. The figures used are those set by the USDA for women between the ages of 18-30.

	Notes	Deficiency Symptoms	Foods that Help
Iron	Important to pay attention to, especially during that time of the month when you will be losing blood and iron levels will dip. Iron is absorbed more easily when consumed with vitamin C (e.g. a glass of orange juice)	Fatigue, inability to concentrate and difficulty in breathing.	Broccoli, spinach, dried fruit (raisins, prunes), seeds and soy products. RDA = 18mg/day
Omega 3 Fatty Acids	Essential for the production of new cells, as well as for allowing the flexibility of cell membranes, which allows them to better absorb nutrients and minerals. Also inhibits the development of cancerous growths and reduces the risk of cancers. Can help regulate hormone levels and serves as a natural anti-depressant, helping to keep your spirits high. It may also be vital for healthy eyesight.	Dry hair, dandruff, and dry skin. Fatigue, poor memory, heart problems, mood swings/depression, poor circulation.	Cold water fish, fortified eggs, canola oil, soybeans, pumpkin seeds, walnuts, flaxseeds, dark leafy greens and fish oil capsules. (*There are vegetarian algae-derive Omega 3 supplements available). RDA = Currently none, though the National Institute of Health recommends adults to aim for about four grams daily.

	Notes	Deficiency Symptoms	Foods that Help
Zinc	As well as strengthening the immune system and playing an important role in shortening the length of the common cold (see page 161), Zinc is good for acne since it controls the skins production of sebum. It also helps prevent osteoporosis (bone loss and weakness) and plays an important role in eye health. On top of all this, it is an important mineral for appetite control AND may increase fertility (hey! You might be thinking about this one day soon...)	Poor sense of taste and smell, poor appetite. Skin rashes, diarrhea, anemia, hair loss. White marks/lines across nails	Beef, turkey, peas, liver, shellfish, chickpeas, beans, nuts. RDA = 8mg/ day
Vitamin C	Great for the skin, a powerful antioxidant, helps protect against UV rays. Will also razor-sharpen your immune system.	Poor wound healing, frequent colds or infections.	Berries, kiwi, bell peppers, tomatoes, broccoli, spinach, grapefruit, and orange (including juice) Vitamin C RDA = 75mg/day
Vitamin B12	Helps regulate stress and controls your mood, as well as increasing your energy levels. It is often lacking in vegetarians (see below.)	Feeling weak, tired, lightheaded. Very pale skin, bleeding Gums. Feeling nauseous, weight loss. Diarrhea & constipation.	Fish, red meat, poultry, milk, cheese, and eggs. Also added to some breakfast cereals. RDA = 2.4 mcg (0.0024 mg)/ day

	Notes	Deficiency Symptoms	Foods that Help
Magnesium	Magnesium supports the immune system, keeps bones strong, regulates blood sugar levels and can reduce period cramps.	Muscle cramps, PMS, anxiety, fatigue, headaches, sleep disorders, low energy.	Find magnesium in green veggies— especially spinach, whole grains (flour, bread, rice), nuts, seeds and legumes. RDA = 320 mg/ day.
Calcium	Calcium helps to keep bones firm, and it is also needed to help the nerves and muscles function. Because it helps muscles contract correctly, receiving adequate amounts may prevent period cramps.	Frequent bone fractures, muscle pain, spasms, PMS. Tingling or numbness in hands and feet	Calcium can be found in milk, and milk products (cheese, yogurt) but also in soy products (check packet), bok-choy, broccoli, and fortified juices. RDA= 1000mg/day.
Vitamin E	Helps tissues to grow healthily; a great antioxidant. Moisturizes skin, improves skin tone, helps heal scars, burns and cuts. Protects against UV damage. Reproduction and anti-aging.	Digestive system problems, tingling in the arms, hands, legs, or feet, liver/ gallbladder problems	Vegetable oil, nuts, leafy vegetables. RDA = 15 mg/day

A Special Note for the Veggies

For vegetarians, there are a few vitamins that are necessary to pay more attention to and ensure that you're getting enough of. In particular B12, which helps with maintenance of the nervous system and thus helps the body deal with the physiological effects of

stress, is often lacking in a vegetarian diet. B12 also essential for the growth of red blood cells. Severe deficiency of B12 can lead to anemia, which will leave you with headaches, fatigue, and sudden blackouts/ fainting if you are menstruating. The Recommended Daily Amount (RDA) is 11 mg. Cereals are often fortified with B12, so check the packet of your cereal and switch it up if it is lacking in B12. Again, a vitamin supplement can help.

Nutrition 30 Day Regime

*Use the shopping list in the back of the book in order to include as many of these **superfoods in your diet** each week. Also, be on the lookout for superfoods on the menu!*

***Invest in a good multivitamin** and remember to take it daily.*

*Up your **water intake.***

*Try switching to **organic foods** gradually if your purse-strings allow it.*

Stomach Trouble

Avoiding Bloating

Bloating is a very unfortunate but common problem for us young ladies. We all have those days when we look down at our stomachs and fear that we might suddenly be three months pregnant judging by the belly-bloat. Fortunately, there are a number of ways to prevent bloating, but if it is too late and you are feeling like a sumo wrestler, never underestimate the power of a loose-fitting dress or a long bohemian top on those days. Try not to let it ruin your social life or your day! There are lots of things you can do to avoid feeling bloated on your wedding day.

The week before the wedding, drink LOTS of water and avoid caffeine and alcohol. One major cause of bloating is water retention, whereby the body tries to hold on to as much water as possible due to the fear of a water shortage. Caffeine, salt and alcohol all dehydrate the body and contribute to water retention. In order to increase the water levels in your body, try to limit your intake of these, as well as refined (white, processed) sugar. Walk around to get your circulation moving and eat protein with every meal—for example lean meat, fish, yogurt, cottage cheese, and so on - this can also calm the stomach.

There are many causes of bloating and/or water retention. Consider if any of the following might be problematic for you:

* Too much salt

* Chewing gum—this causes you to swallow excess air

* Eating when stressed, on the run, upset, too fast, while talking

* Drinking water from a fountain or through a straw

* Constipation (see the next section)

* Weak abdominals

* A food intolerance/Irritable Bowel Syndrome (IBS)

*The average American consumes 3,600-4800 mg of salt a day, which is twice the recommended amount. To reduce your salt intake, put the salt shaker away! Instead, season food with herbs, spices, and non-sodium-based sauces. Always wash anything that comes canned thoroughly (beans, chickpeas, olives), and try to limit your consumption of these foods as much as possible. Use low-sodium soy sauce, and avoid eating out too much where you cannot be in control of your sodium intake. See more on this on page 131.

Many ladies experience bloating post lunch when the abs slack and food expands into the extra space. It might be difficult to fit into your working day, but if you do have the luxury of being a bit wacky at work, a few crunches/sit-ups in the afternoon and making a conscious effort to sit up straight will help!

Foods That Can Cause Bloating

Food Intolerances/IBS

It is beyond the scope of this book to get into the exhausting subject of IBS (Irritable Bowel Syndrome) and other food intolerances, but there are many informative books devoted entirely to these subjects. A list of these books can be found in the appendices. (If these issues affect you, there are many ways in which you can control these irritations, and making the effort to deal with them will be more than worth your while. Please don't suffer in silence—IBS is a nightmare to live with, no matter how embarrassing it is!)

There are many kinds of foods that can on occasion cause digestive irritation in almost everyone.

These are:

❊ Flour products such as potatoes, rice, corn, bread, noodles.

❊ Artificial sweeteners such as Sorbitol, Manitol and Lacitol (as well as others) found in diet drinks and low-calorie yogurt/desserts.

❊ Carbonated drinks—these inhibit the stomachs ability to empty itself effectively.

123

Solutions to Stomach Trouble

1. Avoid problematic food and drinks (see above). Try to identify a pattern when you experience stomach trouble—what might have caused it? Keep a food diary if necessary.

2. Try to cure constipation by upping your fiber levels if you are not regular enough (see page 126)

3. Conversely, if you are too gassy, you might be eating too much fiber at one sitting. For example, a meal consisting of cabbage, root vegetables followed by fruit can give the digestive system too much work.

4. Try probiotics—Yakult or plain yogurt with live culture can do wonders for balancing a dodgy stomach.

5. Sipping tea after a meal—fennel, peppermint, chamomile, fruit, herbal will aid digestion.

6. Eat a light dinner—breakfast like a queen, lunch like a princess, dinner like a pauper.

7. Eat slowly and avoid stressful conversations at the dinner table.

8. Avoid drinks with meals (except water) and practice self-awareness of what you are eating and how much. Some people find keeping a food diary helpful for this purpose.

9. Eat cucumbers! They are excellent at filtering out excessive amounts of water and salt. (This is similar to the way cucumbers work on puffy eyes.)

10. Avoid eating fruit within an hour of mealtimes - consume it alone.

Constipation

While many women are affected by constipation, it is important to know that it is NOT a normal state and should be corrected, not ignored. Severe constipation can wreak havoc on both your health and mind, and ignoring

it can lead to depression, loss of appetite, and even hemorrhoids. It is best to deal with it a.s.a.p. If you are not using the "ladies" most days, take it as a signal that something in your diet or lifestyle needs improving. Winning a battle with chronic constipation will seriously improve your life.

Causes of Constipation

* Dehydration—a lack of water

* Not enough fiber

* Not leaving enough time to use the bathroom in the morning

* An irregular routine

* Uncomfortable/unfamiliar living arrangements/travel

* Stress

* A change in diet

* Low amounts of exercise

* Ignoring the urge to use the bathroom

* Depression

* Laxative abuse (this leads to weakened bowels). If you need to get things moving, try natural laxatives such as prune juice or warm coconut milk. Using over the counter laxatives can be addictive and will result in a vicious cycle as your bowels forget how to move without a chemical stimulant. Not to mention, the associated cramps.

* Medicines (especially pain relievers, anti-depressants, iron pills) may affect the bowels ability to move as they should. Check medicine packets for known side-effects.

Ways to Ease Constipation

Look at your diet to see if you are supplying your bowels with enough roughage—aka fiber. You should be consuming between 25-35 grams a day from fruit, vegetables, cereals, and whole grains. Increase your intake slowly to avoid discomfort (see the example meal plan on page 127).

* Drink more water; your intestines need it! Avoid ice-cold beverages which can inhibit digestion, instead, drink room temperature, lukewarm, and hot beverages.

* Avoid too much coffee as it dehydrates the bowels and acts as a diuretic. (A small amount may trigger a bowel movement, but too much will have the opposite effect.)

* Lower your stress levels. I know, I know, put that on your 'to do' list! Yoga helps ease your mind tremendously and any kind of exercise—even walking for half an hour a day—will help to release stress and get your bowels moving.

* Leave time to go to the bathroom in the mornings.

* Find a bathroom you are comfortable with - preferably a clean, quiet, private one.

* Ginger will help aid digestion and correct constipation. Cook with it, or buy ginger tea for post meals.

A 30 Day Meal Plan To Increase The Amount Of Fiber In Your Diet

During the 30 days before the wedding, you can increase your fiber intake without uncomfortable side effects. If things do become uncomfortable, slow down the following day and listen to your body. Don't forget to drink lots of water as well.

Each week I suggest adding a fiber-rich food to one more of your meals, gradually building up to the recommended 25 grams of fiber every day.

WEEK 1: Every morning, choose a breakfast cereal with a high fiber content (6-8 grams) e.g. bran flakes or raisin bran. Enjoy a sliced banana on top, or a piece of fresh fruit (adding 2-3 grams of fiber).

Cumulative Fiber total: 8-11 grams daily

WEEK 2: For lunch, make a sandwich using 100 percent whole-wheat bread (4 grams of fiber). Add salad leaves of your choice. Eat another piece of fresh fruit or a side of raw vegetables (approximately one cup = 2 grams of fiber).

Cumulative Fiber total: 14-17 grams daily

WEEK 3: For dinner, introduce beans! Add 1/4 cup garbanzo, pinto, or black beans to your regular main dish, be it salad, soup, pasta, or meat and vegetables. Beans will add a nice texture and flavor to most dishes (adds 3 grams of fiber). Also try to include another vegetable: dark leafy greens, carrots, cauliflower, eggplant, asparagus (adds 2-4 grams of fiber).

Cumulative Fiber total: 19-24 grams daily

WEEK 4: Every day, snack on dried fruit (1/4 cup) or nuts (1/4 cup) twice a day mid-morning, mid-afternoon, or pre/post dinner. (adds 4-6 grams of fiber).

Cumulative Fiber total: 23-26 grams daily

Bingo!

Cultural TidBit

Eating slower aids digestion. Kimiko Barber, author of The Chopstick Diet recommends eating all your meals with chopsticks, which will "naturally lead to smaller mouthfuls, reducing the amount of food you eat, and you will eat more slowly, encouraging the flow of digestive juices, leaving you feeling more satisfied and full of energy." If you can't use chopsticks, put your fork down in between bites and make a conscious effort to eat slower.

Making Healthy & Conscious Choices.

"YOU BETTER CUT THE PIZZA IN FOUR PIECES BECAUSE I'M NOT HUNGRY ENOUGH TO EAT SIX."

- YOGI BERRA

Eating Out and Portion Size

If you would like to drop a few pounds, the easiest way to do so and not miss out on your favorite foods is to cut the size of your portions. The likelihood is that you probably won't even miss what's absent from your plate. You see, us humans are animals after all! Animals are programmed to eat whatever is put in front of them. In the wild, you'd never know when the next meal would come or when you might need to use that stored fat in case of famine. As an evolutionary lag, our brains are hard-wired to think that it is best to consume and store those calories while they are available to us. This also explains why we enjoy the taste of sugary, high-fat foods—biologically they are more advantageous to us, and we can use that energy to hunt and kill the next meal.

Except we don't. We most likely walk 30 feet to the fridge, from the car to the grocery store, or at the very most, a few blocks to the restaurant. And you probably know roughly when (and possibly where and what) your next meal will be. And I'm pretty sure that it doesn't involve running around with a bow and arrow in order to track it down and kill it before plonking it on your plate! (though cooking might sometimes involve such exhausting endeavors.)

When we don't expend energy getting our next meal, we get fat. Those calories we consume go unburned and we store them as flab.

Portion size certainly has a big part to play in this. It is well known that portion size has increased dramatically as different companies try to fight for our custom. When I first arrived in the States, I saw a tiny, elderly lady carrying a soft drink around the super market that was bigger than her head. She was using two hands to carry the thing, and sucking through a straw in tiny sips. I have to admit that I found this incredibly funny, but also quite sad at the same time. She didn't need that much fizz—she was probably hyperactive and irritable for a week after drinking it, yet probably just like the rest of us, she was just trying to finish what she was given.

To emphasize the point about calories and portion sizes, the number of calories in a Starbucks Tall (12oz) coffee frappuccino is 181, versus 301 for the Venti (20oz) size. Choose your size carefully and you can still enjoy a "little bit of what you fancy" regularly.

What You Can Do

Stop eating and drinking when you are no longer hungry (I know it's tough, but it can be done), and be conscious of how much food is on your plate. Don't be tempted to put as much food on your plate as your hubby-to-be. Guys should on average be eating 500 calories more a day than us girls (2,500 calories vs. 2,000). If you are going to a restaurant that you know has huge portion sizes, split a main course dish with your friend/fiancé, or order a couple of smaller appetizers instead of a main course.

Eat This, Not That

The incredibly popular book *Eat This, Not That* by David Zinczenko and Matt Goulding was first published in 2007 and has since helped tons of people learn how to lose weight without dieting and without calorie counting. The idea is simple—some foods and restaurant choices can be easily replaced by lower calorie, lower fat options without you even noticing

the difference in taste. The book makes you aware of the hidden calories, fat, and sodium in food and drink choices that you would otherwise have no idea about.

Staying trim is not about missing out or not enjoying your food, but in a society where foods can be loaded with extra calories and fat without us being aware of it, it also takes a bit of strategy to keep our weight down. *Eat This, Not That* aims to educate the general public to make wiser choices, and many restaurant chains have taken notice of this growing awareness and improved some of their overly unhealthy meals or began to offer healthier options. The book provides a realistic approach to weight loss without the need to deprive yourself. I'm a fan. Find out more about the *Eat This, Not That* series in the appendix.

8 Simple Rules to Healthy Eating Out

1. Despite what you might hear, you can still enjoy delicious favorites such as pasta. It's the sauce and toppings you need to watch out for if you want to keep your weight down. Choose red sauces (marinara) over pesto or cream ones (alfredo).

2. Skip the mayonnaise—BBQ sauce, mustard, and ketchup are lower fat choices.

3. Choose thin crust pizza bases over pizza pie and deep crust for fewer calories and carbs.

4. Salads aren't always your healthiest choice - they can pack on a huge calorie, sodium and fat punch. Choose light or fat-free salad dressings over ranch or cheese ones, and ask for them on the side.

5. "Crisp" is usually menu-talk for "fried." "Crispy chicken pieces" really means fried chicken. Since fried food is so high in fat, choose baked and grilled options instead.

6. Don't be afraid to customize the menu. Ask to remove the cheese, hold the bacon or bring the salad dressing on the side. Order salad instead of fries. Most establishments are more than willing to do so if you ask.

7. Split entrees, or just order an appetizer and a side salad if the portion sizes are overly large.

8. Research restaurant menus ahead of time—see below!

Healthy Dining Finder

For an excellent resource on planning your meals ahead of time, try **www.healthydiningfinder.com**. *This site, partially funded by the Center for Disease Control and Prevention, allows you to find healthy choices at all kinds of restaurants across the US so you can know the nutritional analysis of your meal and try to make healthy, informed decisions based on this knowledge. Just type in your zip code and see what healthy options are available near you!*

Snack Attack: Snacking & Why You Should

Snacking gets a bad rap, but it really shouldn't. Some people don't need anything more than 3 square meals a day, others (myself included) prefer smaller meals and lots of nourishment in between. As well as keeping me focused (and interested) at work, I believe that (healthy) snacking is a fab way to keep the metabolic furnace alive!

The key, as always, is balance and moderation. The snacks you choose should aim to keep you going and curb your appetite, not make you sleepy, sluggish, or even hungrier one hour later (as high sugar, low nutrition options will).

So, what should you choose if dinner is at eight, but you just can't wait?

Here are some **Healthy Snack Ideas** from the readers of my blog, <u>www.wowglowingbride.com</u>;

* ✱ "Apples slices with tahini, almond, or peanut butter. They are so good!"

* ✱ "Grilled tofu! Cut up firm tofu into blocks, lie on a baking tray and season with soy sauce and crushed garlic. Bake in the oven for 10 minutes at 300 degrees celsius. Can be eaten hot or cold."

* ✱ "Raw vegetable sticks with hummus, cottage cheese, or low fat cream cheese hits the spot and satisfies the crunchiness I crave"

* ✱ "An apple with a piece of cheese. Cheese is satisfying but limit how much or you won't feel good afterwards."

* ✱ "If it's morning and breakfast didn't fill me up, I'll get a yogurt and drizzle it with honey. Sometimes I'll add granola or nuts to make it more substantial."

* ✱ "Banana and peanut butter—takes me back to being a kid!" (Note: the harder the banana is, the better. It will keep you full for longer!)

* ✱ "I probably should say fruits, vegetables and nuts, but honestly I sometimes snack to brighten up my day. In that case, a square of chocolate or a cereal bar does the job."

* ✱ "Popcorn. I just don't put all the butter on it. Just a tiny bit of olive oil and salt and it is transformed from junk food to health food." (Note: avoid pre-packaged popcorn and make your own.)

❋ "If I'm home, I'll make some edamame. I buy the frozen stuff, boil it for three minutes and season it with chili salt. A bowl of edamame takes much longer to eat than something else I might choose, and it's high in protein so I get satisfied very easily."

❋ " Raisins. I love raisins!!!!" (Note: mix them up with cereal & nuts for a trail mix high in protein!)

Things to Remember When Choosing Your Snacks

– Don't feel bad about snacking. It's okay not to starve all afternoon! In fact, you shouldn't let yourself get overly hungry. This is the key to preventing being tempted into a bad dinner choice or a post-dinner binge.

– If you aren't so hot at the self-control, it's wise to choose something that is portion controlled. Otherwise that apple and peanut butter snack might turn into a 500-calorie meal if you can't put it down.

– Combining complex carbohydrates like whole-grain breads with protein-rich snacks such as low-fat yogurt, cheese, milk, or hummus is going to be the most satisfying option and keep you going. Eating one or the other won't have the same effect.

– Cereal bars can be a good option, but always check the label. Aim for a bar that has around 150 calories, five grams of protein, and less than 7 grams of fat. Otherwise it's just a candy bar in disguise!

Drinks

"WHAT IS THE DEFINITION OF A GOOD WINE? IT SHOULD START AND END WITH A SMILE."

- WILLIAM SOKOLIN

It would be unrealistic for me to tell you not to drink during this time. It is a time for celebration after all. Drinking—in moderation—is encouraged!

As for what to choose, the healthiest alcoholic drinks are the "straight" ones. Dry wines and light beers fit in this category. Red wine is low in carbs, additives, and has some heart-health benefits too. It is advisable to choose wine over sugary cocktails. Cocktails will most likely cause spikes in your blood sugar levels and make you super hungry a few hours later or right into the next day.

Cultural Tidbit

If you needed any more convincing about the benefits of drinking red wine, people from the Mediterranean region who regularly drink red wine, have lower risks of heart disease than the average population. Another reason to heart wine, but remember the golden rule—everything in moderation. A small glass of red wine on a regular basis is okay; half a bottle every other night is not.

What Kind of Wine Should I Choose?

Cabernet has the most antioxidant power of all the red wines out there. Choose the deepest, richest in color and seek out organic wherever possible. While it might be tempting to pick up that bottle of bargain plonk, choosing high-quality alcohol is important. Generally, the more expensive wines have fewer preservatives and will result in less chance of headaches in the morning.

If you prefer to drink white wine over red, dry white wine is less calorific than sweet or medium. Sweet dessert wines are the highest in calories.

If you are watching your weight, avoid creamy alcoholic drinks such as Baileys, Irish coffee, White Russians, Eggnog, as these have a high fat and calorie content.

Top 3 Alcoholic Drink Choices

1. Red Wine (good quality, organic, or at least no sulfites) eg. Pinot Noir

2. White Wine (dry, medium-dry) eg. Sauvignon Blanc, Chardonnay

3. Light beer. Most of the major brands now offer a light brand, though the quality and drinkability ranges from great to terrible. For a decent taste try Amstel Light, Beck's Premier Light, or Budweiser Select.

Non-alcoholic Drinks

Many of us are tricked into believing that diet drinks are 'healthier' than the full calorie versions. This is hard to argue since there is really nothing healthy about artificially sweetened, colored and/or flavored water! While they may contain less calories than their full sugar versions, evidence suggests that dietary drinks actually lead to weight gain. How? By tricking the body into thinking it is receiving energy- the metabolism then rises and your body becomes hungry as a result. It is best to avoid carbonated

drinks—diet and full sugar—as much as possible. Save them for a treat and don't make them a part of your daily life. Your skin, stomach, teeth and mood will all thank you for it!

Smoothies

Synonymous with healthy images and fitness buffs, the concept of the smoothie as a healthy option is a dangerous one. Calories in smoothies vary from 150–600, and fat content from 0g– 30g+!

Some are just called milkshakes by another name, so be careful what you order.

Do's

* Keep it simple—fruits and non-fat/soy milk or yogurt.

* Choose drinks made with real fruit

* Order the smallest size; juice smoothies contain a lot of sugar.

Don'ts

* Don't order drinks made with ice cream, peanut butter, cream, whole milk, syrups, caramel, and chocolate. Sorry!

One Last Thing...Breakfast

Set Yourself Up For a Fabulous Day Everyday

Be sure to make the time or effort for breakfast—it is such a luxury! This is every slim lady's secret. If you make time for breakfast, you are much less likely to get peckish in the afternoon or even mid-morning, as well as giving your metabolism that jolt it needs after a 12 hour fast. You'll feel

less irritated, and less likely to get into the cycle of late-night eating. What might be a chore at first will soon be what gets you out of bed every morning. Cereal with skim milk, toast and eggs, oatmeal, yogurt, granola and fruit…

Plus, breakfast is one of the easiest way to get a great big dose of fiber.

Make sure that you have some good eat-on-the-go commuting options for the days when there is no time for breakfast. Kashi "Go Lean" bars are a good choice. Not all cereal bars are equal. Check the labels very carefully for sugar, protein and fat content as well as preservatives and trans-fats. Anything not providing you with stable energy will result in mood swings and hunger dips, so aim for high protein to keep you full.

30 Day Regime to Overcome Stomach Problems

Eat breakfast to get your system going every morning and avoid over-eating later on in the day.

Increase your fiber intake if necessary

Avoid stomach-bloating foods

Keep an eye on your *portion sizes* and *drink sizes too!*

> ## "Like anyone else, there are days I feel beautiful and days I don't, and when I don't, I do something about it."
>
> ### -Cheryl Tiegs

The Beauty of Exercise

Exercise should not only be performed to lose weight, and this should not be your only motivation (though admittedly it helps.) Exercise is great for the heart, bones, and your mind. It reduces your risk of heart disease and high blood pressure, strengthens your bones and muscles, relieves PMS, lowers stress and improves a bad mood. It can also regulate appetite, blood-circulation, sleep, as well as improving your confidence! If this were a pill we would surely want to take it!

Exercising for Weight Loss

With one month to go until your wedding day, I'm hoping that at this point any major weight loss should be achieved. Losing weight is not an easy thing to do, and I certainly do not advocate a crazy weight-loss regime in the four weeks prior to your wedding. You need to keep your energy levels up and your mind sane, girl!

Rather, to maintain a stable weight or lose those last 1-4 pounds during this time, try your best to exercise regularly, practice portion-control and cut back on sweets and alcohol. No denying yourself, no skipping meals, and be

sure to continue to fuel your body with plenty of vitamins and nutrients. It is super important to keep up your energy levels and immune system at this important stage—it is going to be a busy few weeks!

Toning, however, can most definitely be achieved within 30 days. I can't even begin to count the number of times I have read advice such as "take the stairs instead of the escalator," "get off the bus one stop earlier..." not terrible advice and definitely things you can incorporate into your everyday life. But, we are on a 30-day time limit here, right? So, I vow to focus on those workouts that really do produce miracle results. Most of the recommendations I have included are tried and tested by my most beautiful, fit, sexy, and healthy girl friends, so I have seen the results myself and can guarantee that there was no crash dieting or silly business accompanying the dramatic outcomes.

These DVDs are all designed to produce nice results in 2-4 weeks when done 3-4 times a week. With *Amazon.com* and other online stores offering 3 day shipping, and even the slightly costlier overnight shipping option, you can start tomorrow and achieve that dream booty and arms in no time!

Toning Exercises

1. Pilates—Tight and toned muscles, a longer, leaner physique (especially around the waistline), and reduced stress are just a few of the benefits of Pilates. Pilates also increases energy and helps to improve posture and balance.

- a. **10 Minute Solution: Rapid Results Pilates** ~ Lara Hudson. Makes it easy to fit into your day. Try doing one, two, or three 10 minute sessions each morning or evening.

- b. **Classical Pilates Technique—The Complete Workout Series in English & Spanish** (Modified Basic/Basic/Intermediate/Advanced/ Super Advanced) (2002), Peter Fiasca. Don't be intimidated by the front cover! This is not synchronized gymnastics as it seems to suggest. Rather, it is a series of 16-minute intense workouts using

the classic moves from Pilates. It is not presented in a very "sexy" way (no pearly whites or hot outfits here), but it is a very effective and more traditional approach to the exercise. Because the workouts vary from modified basic to advanced, you can use this DVD way after the wedding to continue and advance your Pilates skills.

2. The Bar Method—(Need hand weights and a chair)

The Bar method is a relatively new workout but the hype sounds promising. Claiming that after about 10 lessons your legs will look longer, your butt will be perkier, your abdominals flatter, and your shoulders, arms, and chest will be defined, it sounds like a dream. It is also claimed that the Bar Method helps burn more fat than its sisters Pilates and Yoga, as it is more intense and you will indeed feel a burn in your thighs the first few times. Highly recommended but certainly not for the faint-hearted - this is a proper workout! Visit the Bar Method website to find out more at **http://www.barmethod.com/**

    a. **The Bar Method Body—Fat Free** by Burr Leonard (50 minutes)

    b. **The Bar Method Accelerated Workout** by Burr Leonard (50 minutes)

3. Callanetics

    a. **Callanetics** 10-Year Younger in 10 Hours.

Okay, so looking 10 years younger may or may not be your desire here, but I would take that title with a pinch of salt. You are not going to lose your wrinkles or suddenly develop dental braces or frizzy hair after completing these workouts. Rather, after 10 hours of workouts, it has been noted that the body's largest muscles will be tightened and firmed. The bust will be lifted and the stomach flattened. It is recommended to follow the 60-minute workout twice a week to see these changes in your body.

4. Power Yoga

    a. **The Firm Power Yoga by Kristen Strohecker**

141

Good for a beginner or if you're not in the best shape of your life. You will see results in about 10 sessions, and it is much more of a workout than most other types of Yoga. It is a fairly painless workout with modified beginner poses. However, if you are quite flexible or advanced and want a more serious workout, I personally recommend option B;

b. Rodney Yee Power Yoga Total Body

Does exactly what it says - total body! And man do I love Rodney! He saved me from some seriously stressful days when I was in an intensive language study program and going out of my mind. And, an additional benefit was the flat stomach I gained while I was at it. This is not for beginners and can leave you out of breath the first few times. The total DVD length is 63 minutes, but of course, as ever, you can cut it off whenever you feel necessary. (30 minutes at a time, 3-5 days a week is a good aim.)

The Toning-While-You-Walk Shoe Craze— What's the Skinny on Them?

You've probably seen the ads - these so-called "toning shoes" hit the market a few years back and claim to help tone your lower body while you workout. The science part is that they create an uneven platform, which forces your muscles to work harder as if you are walking on sand, hence making your workout more challenging.

There are four major brands on the market right now.

1. **MBT**—*The original and most expensive, the technology started in Switzerland. They come with a video to show you how to get 100% effectiveness from your shoe. Priced at over $200, though of course you can find deals.*

2. **Skecher's Shape-ups**—*Claim to improve blood circulation, tighten the butt, tones the abs and the thighs, and strengthen the calf muscles as well as reducing knee joint stress and improving the posture. The style and shape of these shoes leave a lot to be desired.*

3. **Reebok Easy Tones**—*By far the more aesthetically pleasing on the market, they appear almost like normal running shoes and are more reportedly more comfortable. The technology is slightly different to that of the other brands. Rather than forcing the foot forward, Easy Tones have two airpads under the heel and the toe of the foot, which create instability.*

4. **Fitflops**—*started off as flip-flops rather than sneakers, they now come in a variety of styles including boots so you can wear them anywhere. The website claims that they increase muscle activation by 16% due to their 'microwobble midsole' technology.*

Pro's: *Toning Shoes may help to increase the effectiveness of your workout, and make daily chores more beneficial (supermarket, short walks and so on) by adding a challenge to your routine. There's also the possibility that wearing them might reduce cellulite and vein problems, as well as increasing ankle strength when a wearer has suffered from ankle injuries.*

Cons: *There are concerns that this type of shoe might actually cause injuries and be dangerous for anyone with stability problems or tendency to fall over! They are fairly expensive, not particularly attractive and some critics say that they are forcing the body to behave unnaturally.*

143

THE BOTTOM LINE—*this type of shoe is probably not going to make you shed pounds, but they might help your lower half to tone up, and may even encourage you to get out and exercise more, which is never a bad thing.*

Wedding Dress Workouts

Every wedding dress shows off a different part of the body depending on it's style and shape. Here are some exercises I recommend for targeting specific areas of your body to look fantastic in that wedding dress!

Choose what exercises to follow depending on the type of dress you are wearing. If you are new to these kinds of exercises, make sure to pay special attention to the breathing notes. Very often the inhale and exhale instructions are contradictory to our intuition, but are important to follow.

- Always stretch gently to warm up your body.

- Hand-held weights provide resistance and help muscles progress much faster.

- Do these exercises every other day to allow the muscles to rest in between sessions.

- Use 2-5 pound weights depending on your strength and fitness levels.

DRESS TYPE - The Waist-hugging Sheath

What you want: A flat, toned torso

The abs consist of the upper and lower abdominals, as well as the oblique muscles (the sides of your waist). All work in harmony and you should pay attention to all of them to get that flat washboard stomach! Unfortunately standard sit-ups won't hit all of the areas, but these fail-proof stomach will!

1. **Bicycles** - Best for the Upper Abdominals.

1. Lie flat on your back and place your fingertips lightly behind your ears with your elbows extended in either direction.

2. Lift your right arm up to a 40° angle from the floor, and at the same time bring your left knee in toward you.

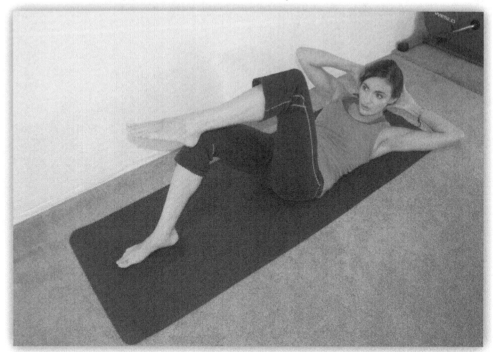

3. Aim to touch your right elbow to your left knee, but only go as far as you can without straining.

4. Gently lower to the floor and repeat on the other side (left elbow to right knee).

5. Do this slowly and in a controlled, flowing motion. Aim for 10 on each side (a total of 20) and 1-3 sets depending on your ability.

2. The Scissors - Best for Lower Abdominals.

1. Lie on your back with your arms either next to you or underneath your butt.

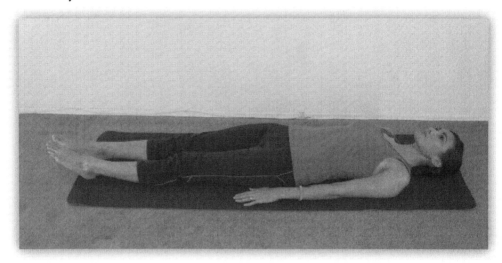

2. Lift your feet a few inches off the ground, making sure that your lower back maintains contact with the floor and does not arch.

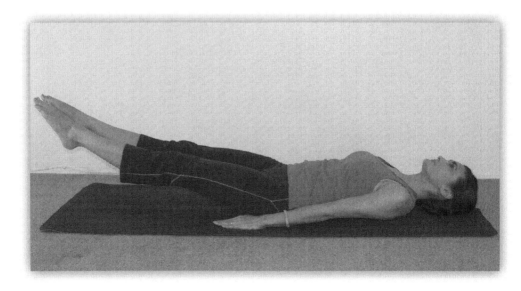

3. Raise your legs (either straight or slightly bent) a few inches off the ground, exhale and begin to cross one leg in front of the other, all the while raising your legs higher and higher. Be sure that your back maintains contact with the ground. Inhale and bring your legs down to the mat, repeating this scissor-like crossing motion. Do 8-10 reps (1 up and down equals 1 rep).

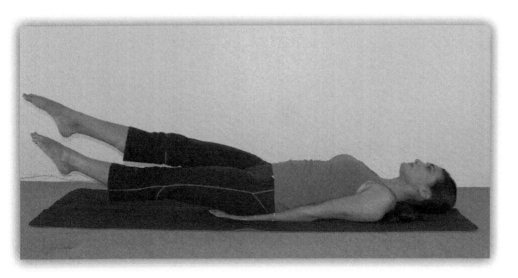

3. The Plank - Best for the Obliques.

1. Lie face-down on your mat.

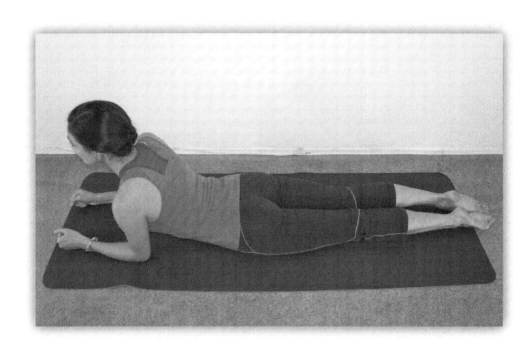

2. Come to the "plank" position by supporting yourself with your forearms and toes. Elbows should be directly under your shoulders at a 90° angle, and your feet should be together. Your back should be flat and parallel to the floor. Be careful not to raise your butt up to the ceiling and try to keep your position solid.

3. Pull your abs in tight, and breathe while holding the pose.

4. Start by holding this position for 30 seconds, then work up to 60 seconds and longer if you can manage. As well as being great for the obliques, the plank is excellent at targeting the lower abs, thighs, and butt.

DRESS TYPE - The Open-back

What you want: An upper-back and shoulder workout

The Reverse Fly

1. Sit on a chair or bench with your knees bent and a dumbbell in either hand.

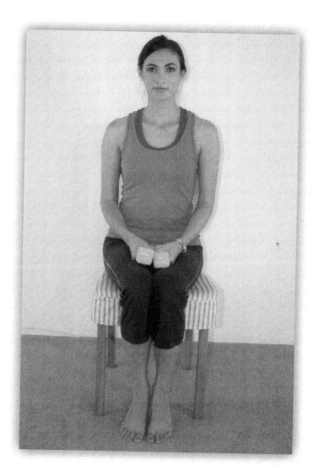

2. Lean forward with your arms hanging next to your legs.

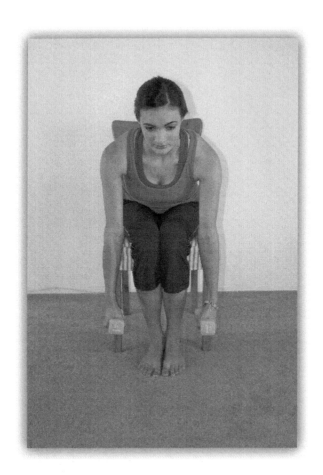

3. Slowly raise the weights up until your arms become level with your shoulders.

4. Slowly lower them back down without hunching or arching your back.

Do this with control and without swinging for 10-15 reps.

DRESS TYPE - Strapless

What you want: Toned triceps (back of your arms) and biceps (front)

Triceps

Circles—

1. Stand feet hip-width apart and hold your arms out straight on either side with your weights.

2. Circle 20 times forward with your palms facing the ground. Then turn your palms to face upward and circle 20 times backwards.

Repeat 2-3 sets. May also be performed without weights.

Overhead Extensions—

1. Assume either a standing or sitting position and hold one weight over your head using both hands.

2. Keeping your elbows close to your head (and taking special care not to whack yourself on the back of the head!) lower the weight behind you slowly and carefully.

3. Once you have reached the lowest position possible, bring it back to the starting position and repeat.

Biceps

1. Bar Bell Curl—

1. Hold a weight in front of you, with your palms facing upwards, and your elbows stuck firmly to your side.

2. Slowly bring the weight up toward your chest—squeeze your biceps and release.

3. Lower the weight back down with control and grace.
Do 3 sets of 10 on each side.

2. **Alternate Dumb Bell Curl—**

1. Stand with your feet shoulder width apart and hold your weights at your side.

2. Take the right arm and bring it up to your chest, palms facing down.

3. Once you get close to your chest, turn the weight so that your palm faces toward you.

4. Bring the weight back down and turn the weight as you go until it is in the position you began with. Repeat with the left arm and do 2 sets of 10 with each arm.

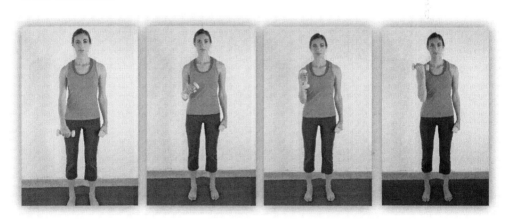

Working Out For Life

While it is fairly easy to stick to an exercise program for four weeks—particularly with a big goal in mind such as your wedding day—to ensure that you stay healthy for life, you should try to adopt health and fitness as a lifestyle and not as something you have to do to get skinny for your sister's wedding, your friend's big birthday party, or your bikini vacation!

There are two things you can do to find an exercise that you will stick to for life. One is ensuring that you do exercise that you enjoy—truly enjoy—in fact, actually get peed off if you have to skip it. The second thing is to adapt your mindset so that your desire to do the exercise is genuine and not a chore. Anytime you attach a negative association to a task—be it work,

cooking, cleaning, working out—you've already stopped enjoying it before you even started. If you seriously enjoy the exercise and adopt a positive viewpoint, you can, and will, make it a habit for life.

I used to hate working out - that was when all I knew was running and hitting the gym. Now I avoid both and practice yoga and walk my dog daily instead, both of which I love and don't dread (most of the time!). "Exercise" has come a long way since the days of running around a sports track or following an aerobics instructor dressed in some funky leotard. Try pole dancing, hiking with your hubby-to-be, Pilates, power walking with your iPod, tai-chi, mountain climbing, beach volleyball. Anything that doesn't feel like exercise first, but is a side effect of fun will mean that you are more likely to stick with it. And enlist your bestest friends to join you so that you don't feel as though your social life is slacking too. Beginning an exercise program with a friend or loved one is one of the most effective ways to ensure that you stick with it.

Your 30 Day Regime for Exercise

- *Choose something you enjoy* and can realistically fit into your existing schedule.

- *Aim for 30 minutes a day.*

- *Use the exercises listed in the section above to **work on your target areas** to match your dress-type.*

- *Mix up your routine so that you don't get bored.*

Avoiding Colds & Flu

Before writing this guide, I met with plenty of brides-to-be, as well as newly weds as part of my research. One of the questions I asked was "What is/was your biggest fear on your wedding day?" Over anything else (well apart from the big red zit which we covered in the first section), brides feared being ill or "under the weather" on their wedding day. Not at all surprising, I was having nightmares about this myself, particularly as I seemed to be surrounded by sick friends and family!

While you can't have complete control over your immune system, you can certainly take some preventative measures, reduce your symptoms—if any—and lessen the time that an illness sticks around for. The key here is early detection of any problems- don't ignore early symptoms and try to listen to your body.

Preventative Measures for Cold and Flu

* Turn off the A/C and open windows instead.

* Most viruses spread through direct contact, so avoid touching your face. Viral bugs can enter through your eyes, mouth, and nose.

* Wash your hands for 20 seconds with warm water and an antibacterial soap regularly, especially after shaking hands, handling money, or returning home. It's not surprising that infections spread like wildfire when you consider that we share doorknobs, computer keyboards, ATMs, and money with others.

* Carry an antibacterial soap or hand gel in your purse and use it regularly when out and about. Obviously, the more people there are in an area, the more germs and viruses there are.

What to Do if You Have Symptoms

* Suck zinc lozenges. Zinc of any kind, but especially in lozenge form, can reduce the severity of your illness if taken within 48 hours of the first symptoms. It may be worth keeping some of these in stock "just in case!"

* Sip chicken soup or other warm liquids - Mom was right about this one.

* Rest! Work with your immune system and not against it. Stay warm and have an early night—this can work major miracles.

* Drink lots of fluids to keep you hydrated and ensure that your body is functioning at it's optimum.

* Blow your nose regularly. This can help dispel your germs rather than sniffing mucus back into your body. Be careful not to do this too aggressively as you can trigger ear and headaches this way.

* Echinacea is an herbal remedy that has been used for centuries as it is thought to boost the action of the immune cells, though the evidence supporting this is still shaky. Purely anecdotal evidence suggests that echinacea can be effective at shortening the length of a cold. (Avoid if you have asthma as it may worsen your symptoms.)

* Other natural remedies include garlic, lemon, honey and menthol. Use them in your cooking or choose teas that contain these ingredients.

PMS

~~Pissy Mood Syndrome~~

~~Pimples Might Surface~~

~~Phat Mid Section~~

Pre-Menstrual Syndrome

"WOMEN COMPLAIN ABOUT PREMENSTRUAL SYNDROME, BUT I THINK OF IT AS THE ONLY TIME OF THE MONTH THAT I CAN BE MYSELF."

ROSEANNE BARR

1. Menstrual Pain

Urg. I am sure by now that you have come up with your own way of dealing with period pain, be it lying in bed with a hot water bottle and back-to-back episodes of Sex and the City, an energetic dance class, or several painkillers and a cup of tea. Everyone handles it differently, and there is no universal way of coping with cramps and physical discomfort.

Perhaps you rarely get period pains, but stressful periods of time (such as wedding planning) are a different story and trigger a monster. There are several things you can try to reduce your symptoms, feel better, and get on with your busy life. Find out which way works for you (and remember it!)

✱ Be sure to load up on Calcium and Magnesium

The Science Part—One of magnesium's many roles is a muscle relaxant. This is especially important for women who suffer from menstrual cramps because cramps are caused by excessively strong contractions of the uterus (womb). Magnesium helps the powerful uterine muscles relax, and thus reduces cramping.

Magnesium's muscle-relaxing powers also help relieve the PMS or menstrual headaches that many women experience.

Unfortunately, many people in the US are magnesium deficient, so keep an eye out for it! Leafy vegetables, nuts, seeds, and soy products are all good sources of magnesium, otherwise try a supplement.

* Avoid ice and anything below room temperature. Basically, try to keep your stomach and body warm by steering clear of ice cream, ice drinks, and not wearing enough layers in cold weather. This is something Chinese medicine teaches and several Asian friends of mine swear by.

* Similarly, apply heat to the abdomen, lower back, or anywhere wear the cramps are setting in. You can use a hot water bottle or heat pads to ease discomfort and help with cramping.

* Try gentle exercise—a walk, some light dancing or yoga. (Avoid the upside down yoga positions, however, when you are menstruating. They always tell you that in yoga class. I have never been so embarrassed in my life when my yoga instructor asked those who were menstruating to sit out at the front. Well, only myself, out of a class of 30, moved to the front. I guess everyone else knew to stay away "that" week!)

* Take some painkillers and drink plenty of room temperature (not ice)water.

* Make sure your iron levels are up. Low iron levels increase your risk of passing out, feeling dizzy or faint.

2. Bloating/Breast Tenderness

During the week leading up to your period, it is not uncommon to gain excess weight—up to 5 pounds and an extra inch or so around the stomach and boobs. This is due to water retention and hormonal changes. The advice here is the same as on other bloat-causing occasions:

* ✸ Exercise gently

* ✸ Drink plenty of water

* ✸ Avoid salty food

* ✸ Take probiotics to aid digestion

* ✸ Drink peppermint or fennel tea

* ✸ Avoid carbonated drinks

* ✸ Avoid caffeine and alcohol before and during your period

* ✸ Eat lots of fresh fruit and veggies

For breast tenderness, some women find evening primrose oil to reduce pain and inflammation. It can found in oil or capsule form, from health stores.

3. Spots

Even those with the clearest of complexions can be affected by those dear lady hormones that catch us this time of the month. They get as excited as your mother-in-law would if she thought you were having a baby. The hormone levels shoot up...and fall right back down when they realize your egg has been left unfertilized. This hormonal roller coaster can take a huge toll on the skin. To try to ease these hormonal fluctuations and be sure to load up on Vitamins A and D, drink LOADS of water, and stay clear of processed foods.

4. Mood Swings

80 % of women admit to having mood swings or mood roller coasters every month— the kind that mean you are on top of the world and super duper happy one moment and vulnerable and depressed the next. It is not fun. Blame those pesky hormones. Here are the top 3 things you can do to stabilize your mood during your period:

* Eat right—the aim here is to eat foods that boost serotonin levels and improve your mood. Think complex carbohydrates (whole grains, brown rice, brown bread, wheat) and avoid simple sugars (white bread, cookies—reduce your sugar intake in general.) Avoid caffeine and alcohol as much as possible, they can play havoc with hormones.

* Exercise—release those endorphins! Exercise reduces your stress and boosts your mood.

* Reach out for emotional support. Your friends and family might be stepping on eggshells around this time or trying to avoid you completely, but let them know what you are going through and that you are trying your best to control your emotions but that you are finding it hard. Women need emotional comfort and support, so a hug here and there, a meaningful conversation, or just some company can ease your irritability.

If you are still suffering from severe physical and emotional distress due to your period, then you might be among the 3-8% of unlucky babes who suffer from what Doctors have labeled PMDD—Pre Menstrual Dysphoric Disorder. PMDD is similar to PMS but much more severe and extreme. It is certainly worth consulting with your MD if you suspect your monthly symptoms are worse than normal.

Part III

Well-Being

> **"A GOOD LAUGH AND A LONG SLEEP
> ARE THE BEST CURES IN THE DOCTOR'S BOOK."**
>
> **IRISH PROVERB.**

*C*o-ordinating a huge party? **Stressful**.

Trying to please **all** of your friends and family? A **Nightmare**.

Doing both of the above while confronting your own identity, emotions and lifestyle changes? **We must be crazy!**

It's no secret that preparing for a wedding and a marriage is physically and emotionally draining. HOWEVER! Although stress, sleep-deprivation, and emotions are very real, you do have one choice that you can make here and now. Pledge to yourself to handle this month's stress in the best way that you possibly can. Look after yourself physically and mentally, remind yourself regularly that things always work out, and be adaptable. Finally, treat everyone who you come into contact with the respect that they deserve. This includes vendors, friends, family, AND your fiancé! Just because this is your day doesn't mean that the world centers around you and no one else has feelings.

 Take the anti-Bridezilla pledge today!

Sleep

"A RUFFLED MIND MAKES A RESTLESS PILLOW."

-CHARLOTTE BRONTË

We all suffer lapses in the quality of our sleep at some point in our lives, and the period before the wedding is a common time to experience this. I certainly spent a few nights tossing and turning over details that I had no reason to worry about in the end.

There is nothing worse then lying in bed feeling absolutely exhausted and waiting to fall asleep...but it just won't happen! If you are having trouble getting to sleep this month, remind yourself that sleep problems at this time are quite common and that you are certainly not alone. It is important not to get upset or frustrated as you can turn anxiety and associated sleep deprivation routine into a vicious cycle.

The science of sleep is very complex, but there are several things you can do to aid the process.

In The Evenings; Winding Down Before Sleep

- **Think your day through** and all of it's events. Talking over dinner with a friend or loved one, or thinking about the day quietly with yourself will allow you to make sense of the day and tie up any loose ends in your mind.

- **Plan ahead for tomorrow** well in advance of bedtime. This way you won't take your problems and thoughts to the bedroom. Write down your niggling to-do's and make lists!

- Use the evening to wind down from work - **avoid doing any activity that stimulates the brain** for 60 minutes before sleeping. Watching TV or speaking with a chatty friend on the phone late at night will get your brain excited and unable to relax. Save your chats for lunchtime or earlier on in the evening.

  • Gentle **yoga or stretching** in the evenings will help your body slow down and relax, but aerobic exercise can increase your energy levels and prevent sleep.

  • **Baths are good** in the evening, but showers are not. They will get your circulation going and wake you up. Also try to avoid bathing within an hour of going to bed because if you are too hot you will find it difficult to sleep.

  • **Warm milk and socks** can help send you into a slumber. It might sound like advice your Gran would give you, but there is nothing worse than having cold feet to keep you awake!

  • **A few walnuts before bedtime** can help you to fall asleep due to their production of melatonin—a hormone produced by the pineal gland which is involved in inducing and regulating sleep. Just don't overdo it or else you'll be awake from indigestion!

At Bedtime

- Hit the sack **when you feel sleepy,** and not before. "Forcing yourself" to fall asleep is often counterproductive and you may create a sleeping problem.

- Try to **keep a consistent bed routine** during the four weeks before the wedding. Keep the same bedtime and same wake-up time each day. You can be a little flexible on the weekends, but don't lie in bed until 11am if you are usually up at 7. (Tempting as it is!)

- **Keep an eye on the room temperature**. Hot rooms will have you tossing and turning, while too much A/C might be keeping you alert. (Ever wondered why the A/C is on high in the movie theatre?)

- **Take a look at the pillow you are using**. If you tend to sleep on your side, your pillow will need to be firmer. If you sleep on your back, the pillow should be flatter. Stomach sleepers need very flat pillows. Figuring out what works for you will improve the quality of your sleep.

When Sleep Doesn't Come

Sometimes it doesn't matter how hard you try to get a good night's sleep—you avoided caffeine, wound down before bed, drank your chamomile tea—some things can keep you awake at night and cause you to toss and turn. Here is what the sleep experts recommend for a happy slumber:

1. **Follow the 15 minute rule:** If you can't sleep after 15 minutes, get up, and do something relaxing until you start to feel sleepy.

2. **Don't worry too much about tomorrow** and your performance. You should be able to cope pretty well after one night's bad sleep; it shouldn't hurt you too much. Try your best to not watch the clock.

3. **When you start to feel sleepy**, (and not before), return to bed.

If that doesn't work...

4. **Write down what's bothering you**: Get up, go to another room, grab your pad and paper and write down anything that is bothering you. Let your subconscious run wild. Then think about how to tackle these issues. Once you have a mini action plan written down, tell yourself that you have dealt with all you can for now, and that you are not going to worry about it again until the morning.

Sleep-Enemies

Caffeine: Okay, I love it too, but I do try to avoid it after 11am. By doing this, caffeine gets me through the day and is out my system by 11pm when I'm thinking of hitting the sack.

Alcohol is another drink that will disrupt your sleep. It might make you sleepy at first, but your sleep will be lighter and more fragmented throughout the night. You might find yourself waking up at random times and left to feel exhausted the morning after.

Exercising before bed. This will give you too much energy by sending oxygen to your brain, which keeps you awake. Exercising in the morning or up until late afternoon is a better idea.

Heavy dinners. Aim to finish eating a light dinner four hours before bed to allow ample time for digestion.

Sugar at night, including in drinks.

Smoking—Avoid within four hours of sleep as nicotine is a stimulant.

Medicines—headache medications can be stimulants too. Check the package for side effects, and discuss with your MD if you feel they may be causing you sleepless nights.

Tight-fitting clothing—you want to be as comfortable and relaxed as possible in bed.

> # "THE BEST BRIDGE BETWEEN DESPAIR AND HOPE IS A GOOD NIGHT'S SLEEP."
>
> ## - E. JOSEPH COSSMAN

How Much Sleep Do We Need?

There is no magic number for the amount of sleep people need, and as you have probably noticed if you look around at friends and family, sleep needs are individual. Some friends might be surviving pretty well off four hours while others may need as many as 10 or more hours to be happy!

These numbers vary for many reasons—age comes into it, as well as health, physical, and mental activity. The general understanding though is that between 7-9 hours per night on a regular basis is normal and healthy. Anything less or more than this can be detrimental to our daily performance, mental, and physical health.

Sleep Debt

While 7-9 hours is the recommended amount of sleep over time for optimum performance (known as "basal sleep"), the amount of sleep one needs on any given night may increase if one has suffered from a bad night's sleep or had a late night in previous days. Scientists have labeled this as "sleep debt," and eventually your body will demand that you pay back this debt with an extra hour or two of sleep. This explains those days when we really find it hard to get up or feel particularly sleepy mid-afternoon during that boring meeting.

A good night's sleep will help you focus, concentrate, and handle situations much better. Not to mention, you'll be a much sweeter person to be around!

Oh, and expect to have bizarre wedding-related dreams; it is normal and most people do! Your brain is just trying to process all of the information it is dealing with during the day in its own funny way. It doesn't mean that your Maid of Honor is going to turn up stark naked or that your cake is going to be a giant pumpkin. I had several of these strange dreams and now the wedding is over, I miss their weird and wonderfulness!

Next we'll look at how to relax and manage stress, which is a major factor in sleeping disturbance.

Relaxation/Managing Stress

"To keep the body in good health is a duty... otherwise we shall not be able to keep our mind strong and clear."

- Buddha

Stress

Though fun at times, wedding planning can also be an incredible source of stress. There are several decisions to be made, a budget to be adhered to, expectations to live up to, and you may or may not be faced with the disappointment of friends and family whom you feel are not pulling their weight in the planning process.

The term "Bridezilla" was coined for a reason—you might be a super duper lovely gal in "real life" but the pressure, extra workload, and expectations of others may lead to you to be uncharacteristically emotional.

Disagreements with both the men and women in our lives (mother, mother-in law, bridesmaids, fiancé) are not uncommon during this time. Try your best to stay centered. Now, this may sound a bit shocking but...**the wedding itself is not really all that important (gasp!). What does matter is the marriage that follows it.** Remind yourself of this regularly. It's dangerous to place all of your hopes and dreams on the wedding day itself— you should be extending your passion and energy into the thousands of days that come afterwards—creating an awesome, happy, marriage, maintaining old friendships and working on the new ones that your marriage has created (his family and friends). Don't let one day jeopardize this!

Having some degree of stress is generally not a problem, and we can often benefit from it to keep ourselves motivated and on top of things. This is referred to as "Eustress"—the healthy kind of stress. Too much stress or the wrong kind, however, is bad for both mind and body.

Everybody copes with stress in different ways. Some may seemingly take it in their stride, while others feel overwhelmed and hopeless. Often, the major difference between these two approaches is the ability to **recognize why and what is causing the stress**. Recognizing the cause leads to learning how to deal with the problem and finding appropriate solutions. In order to keep stress under control, it is important to be able to do the following:

1. **Recognize when you are feeling stressed**. This is not as easy as it sounds! You may have subtle telltale signs such as breaking out, stomachache, a desire to binge eat or drink alcohol, or a sudden desire to clean the house. Everybody's signs of stress are different, but being aware of what your signs are is extremely important.

2. **Recognize what is causing you the stress.** We expect the source to be glaringly obvious to us, but sometimes it is not. You might be subconsciously denying that whatever it is is bothering you. Try to consider every possible cause, perhaps using a pen and pencil to brainstorm, or a friend to shoot ideas off. You might be surprised! There will be times when you can't work out what is stressing you out. That's okay too. It will come to you eventually.

3. **Figure out how to do something** about those stressors that you have some control over. Obviously, a death in the family or an illness cannot be controlled. But other problems such as an uncooperative bridesmaid, a budget spiraling out of control, or a mother-in-law with unreasonable demands can be tackled hands-on.

4. **Learn constructive and healthy ways of reacting to stress**. Talking, cleaning, exercising, cooking, and so on are healthy ways. Binge eating, binge sleeping or biting your nails to the core are not. Make an effort to focus on the former and avoid the latter.

Signals of Stress—Not as Obvious as You Might Think

While there are very obvious signs of stress, the body can also react to stress in less obvious and surprising ways. If you are experiencing any of these symptoms, they may well be indicative of unconscious forms of stress:

- *Sleep problems*

- *Digestive issues*

- *Headaches and migraines*

- *Tiredness*

- *Mood swings*

- *Worse period pains than usual (your hormones are out of whack)*

- *Odd/bad dreams or nightmares.*

- *Persistent gum disease/bleeding gums*

- *Craving of chocolate/sugar (more than usual)*

If you are experiencing these symptoms of **too much stress**, make an effort to tackle the problems head-on to see what you can do to minimize your stress load.

What You Can Do to Reduce Stress

❋ Talk to someone. Your partner, your Mom, your best friend, your bridesmaids, or even someone you don't know particularly well.. A study at the University of Michigan found that simply connecting with a friend increases a woman's progesterone levels, which in turn reduces anxiety and stress. And, we all know the saying "a problem shared is a problem halved." As well as getting a load of your chest, the other person might suggest simple ways around your problem that you are failing to see.

* If the idea of having the "perfect" wedding is what is stressing you out, you might need to re-consider what your idea of the "perfect" wedding is, and whether all the stress involved in planning is detracting from that ideal. Try to think about the long-term marriage you are entering rather than this one day of your life.

* Don't be afraid to delegate some tasks that are not yet completed. You have not failed if you need to ask for help. People are often flattered to be asked and more than willing to lend a hand.

* Some things will go wrong on your day! Accept this fact gracefully and know that it will make your day more personal and memorable. Laugh about it. I am a firm believer that a little imperfection is what creates perfection.

* Write lists! Use your schedule, computer, or phone to set yourself reminders and try as hard as possible to stick to them. Don't beat yourself up if you don't - reschedule them and stay proactive.

* Don't be afraid to say "no" to social occasions. People understand that you are overly busy at this time.

Things to Do to Avoid Stress During This Month

* **Look after number one** (that's you!!) Treat your body in the same way that you would want your loved ones to treat themselves. Get enough sleep, exercise daily, drink plenty of water, eat a sensible diet, don't starve yourself or over exercise, get outside every day, avoid too much alcohol, caffeine, sugar, and tobacco. As always, everything in moderation!

* **Talk to your friends**. Communicate as much as possible. Don't give up your social life. Conversely, don't overdo your social life.

* **Spend time with your partner** and make sure that it is quality time. Firmly schedule this time, and stick with it.

* **Treat yourself** to a massage, a good book, a movie or a yoga class. Go to the salon, window-shop, walk. Connect with yourself and your feelings.

* Write down your thoughts in a **diary or blog.**

* **Meditate.**

* It's worth saying again -**exercise!** Release some endorphins! Merely the fact that you accomplished getting out there and running/walking/gymming will make you feel more on top of things and in control.

If you think you are experiencing levels of stress that are higher than usual, and are connected to your feelings about entering a marriage rather than the wedding day itself, see the section on "Pre-Wedding Blues."

I have also included a list of relaxation tools to find more creative ways of managing your stress levels. Refer to it throughout the month or when you are in need of a pick-me-up.

30 Relaxation Tools That Never Fail

* Working out

* Music—tune into **www.lastfm.com** or **www.pandora.com** for free radio.

* Take a walk. Take a friend, your iPod, or your phone and call a friend.

* Get near water—a river, stream, the ocean. Take your pad and paper, sketchbook, or a camera.

* Call an old friend

* Play with babies/children

* Get outside.

✱ Dance

✱ Play a game or puzzle—cell-phone game, board game, cards, sudoku.

✱ Meditate. Lie on your back with your hands on your stomach and breathe deeply for 5-10 minutes.

✱ Stretch. This. Feels. Great!

✱ Practice yoga

✱ Read a book—an old favorite or some new fiction.

✱ Watch a funny sitcom/movie. Rent your favorite chick flick.

✱ Light candles and enjoy the atmosphere they create.

✱ Give yourself a pedicure—"me" time is good time.

✱ Take a shower or bath and use a relaxing shower gel or bubble bath.

✱ Scrapbooking/make a vision board.

✱ Paint, draw, write. Doing anything creative will lift your spirits.

✱ Make a cup of tea and drink it outside.

✱ Bake—find recipes online.

✱ Listen to songs from your school days or a nostalgic era.

✱ Paint your nails.

✱ Go to a new neighborhood or place of interest. Take pictures.

✱ Go to a coffee shop with a book

✱ Visit a bookstore and browse.

✱ Walk the dog.

* Look through old photos.

* Do the dishes/clean/tidy up.

* If possible, take a day or a half-day off, and do what you really want to do. Don't feel guilty about it, just enjoy it. You will feel so great afterwards.

Worries

Everybody worries sometimes, but some people simply worry more than others.

A worry is a repetitive negative thought about the future-a thought that gets stuck in your mind, like a broken record on repeat. You are unable to do much else besides worrying, even though simply thinking about this outcome that may or may not happen is fruitless.

The very fact that this negative thought is about the future confirms that these thoughts are guesses, predictions, and unfounded ideas that are based on the limited information we have available to us. We are the ones that make them negative—we imagine the worse case scenario.

Typically, worries come in the form of "What if?" "What if" the worst thing possible happened? We want to answer this question and go through all of the possible outcomes. The thought spins through your mind non-stop and you can never get past it.

The important thing to know is that worrying is often an unproductive and non-constructive way to deal with situations. By focusing on the most negative outcome possible, you are jumping to a conclusion, fortune-telling, and undermining your ability to cope with the situation in the way that you probably could and will. You have probably been wrong about this sort of thing in the past, and the likelihood is that you are making "much ado about nothing."

But that is not the best advice if you are in the thick of a worry and this same repetitive thought refuses to leave your mind. If you find yourself worrying excessively, try the following exercise.

How Should You Deal With Worries?

* Firstly, keep the above in mind—this scenario that you are imagining is the worst-case. You have the ability to avoid this in most situations.

* Remind yourself of situations in the past where you have worried endlessly and in the end it was totally fruitless and unnecessary. Learn from these experiences.

* Think about what you would tell your best friend or sister. If she was in your situation this would give you a much more objective outlook. Step away from your situation and look at the facts through these eyes. Are you really justified in your worries from that angle?

* Write worries down and then write down all of the outcomes including the positive or neutral ones. Then come up with ways to avoid or minimize the impact of potential negative outcomes. Aim to turn your worries into productive action.

* Set aside a specific time and location to do your worrying. Don't carry worries around with you all the time otherwise they will truly eat into your work quality, ability to relax and your interactions with other people. This in turn will lead to more problems and more worries.

Productive & Unproductive Worries

Some worries can be useful and productive—they can get our butts into gear! For example, say I am worried about what to do for my birthday. I can use my productive worrying to kick me into action—I can make a reservation at my favorite restaurant, contact some friends telling them to save the date and book a manicure beforehand. Then I can stop worrying about it. However, if I am worried that it is going to rain on my birthday or that I won't get any cards…well I can't do anything about that. This kind of worrying is unproductive. All I can do is write down how I can best deal with these situations if they occur and remind myself that they may not! (and if they did it wouldn't be the end of the world).

Worry Time

Set aside 30 minutes during the day (at least three hours before bedtime.) Sit down, write out your worries, the possible outcomes and ways you can deal with them. If you have worries at any other time of the day, jot them down on a piece of paper or in your phone, and then tell yourself that you will deal with them later during your specified "worry time." Worrying can wait, and knowing that you are going to address it later should calm you. This way it won't interfere with the rest of your day.

Use this space to write down any unproductive worries you may have and for constructing your action plan:

Common Issues for the Bride-to-be

Some of you won't have some—or any—of these problems, and can skip this section entirely. Other's may read about an issue and find that it resonates strongly with you. This is no coincidence; being engaged and getting married bring up the same issues over and over for women from all backgrounds and walks of life. That is just the way it is my friend.

Family Issues

Jealous/Sad or Uninterested Siblings

Getting married can cause all sorts of strange feelings for your brothers, and, in particular, sisters. Perhaps they are not married yet, and seeing you get married is instilling a sense of urgency or making them worry that they are running out of time.

Another possibility is that he or she is feeling a sense of abandonment. From their shoes, it seems as though you are choosing to start a new family, and all of those days of hanging out as a family or going on vacation are over. Holidays will never be the same, and your hubby will always be around as far as they are concerned. They worry they are losing you.

Ideas: *Be kind, be aware. Don't ignore the friction that is happening between you—wait for a good time and talk to them. When you are both relaxed and getting on well, ask if there is something bothering them and show them that you are sincere about wanting to know. Reassure them that you are still you and don't want things to change between you. Talk to them about how they are feeling and about things you can do together in the future, perhaps even planning for a day trip or short vacation if you can.*

Your Parents Don't Like Him

This is a difficult but not uncommon situation. It may not be that they don't like him, rather that he wasn't the kind of guy they envisioned you with, or that they preferred an ex boyfriend.

Ideas: *It may simply take your parents some time to warm up to him, and just let it run it's course if this is the case. In the meantime, you can help things along by making sure that they get to know him and all of the things you love about him. Engage*

them in some bonding activities together, or if he is from a different culture or background, introduce them to that so they can understand more of where he is coming from. Additionally, sometimes all it takes is to hear from you (in a non-aggressive or non-argumentative way) how happy he makes you and that your feelings are firm. If your best interests are what is important to them, this will be enough for them to warm to him too.

Note: If there is a valid reason for them disliking him, e.g. he is rude, disrespectful, or violent, you may want to pay attention to your parents' feelings. Their feelings might be the alarm bells you need, now.

Your Mother is Acting Strange

Keeping in mind that this is a really strange time for her, it is no surprise when Mom gets all weird on you. She may be acting all odd, snap at you, or adopt some other strange behavior. She is stressed out too, and if she is hosting the wedding then she has extra reason to be, on top of the feeling that her 'little girl is growing up'.

Ideas: *You must talk to her. Show her that you are on top of things and that the most important thing to you is that everybody enjoys themselves on the day. If she has any concerns about the wedding or the marriage, talk them through with her. She may be feeling the same sense of loss that your siblings might (see section above), so just assure her that you and her aren't going to drift apart. Again, having dates in the calendar post-wedding can ease any anxiety she feels about post-wedding life.*

You Have Divorced Parents Who Don't Get Along

Of course it would be great if your parents could just get along on your day, even for a few hours, but sometimes this doesn't look likely.

Ideas: *Ask them both to keep your wishes in mind—to act maturely and respectfully to each other—and remind them how much this would mean to you. One thing to keep in mind is seating arrangements—make sure to talk to them a few weeks in advance—who do they want to sit with and where? If they both want to sit with you but can't, sit them at tables equally close to the head table. If they can get along and sit together for a few hours, great. Just don't leave this detail until the day before the wedding because it will stress you out. Have it planned by consulting both of your parents in advance.*

Friends

Friends Don't Want to Hear About It!

Have you been guilty of eating, walking, talking, sleeping Wedding? As tempting as it is, try to avoid talking about your wedding plans 24/7 with your friends. When you see them, wait for them to bring it up. I am sure they are excited, but they have their own lives going on—remember to ask them about that too!

Ideas: *That one person who is genuinely interested in hearing all of the tiniest details and updates—your Mom, Mother-in-law, sister, bridesmaid—save the details for her.*

Feeling Disconnected to Single Girl Friends

Your relationship may or may not change with your single friends, but regardless, they may worry that it will. Hearing that you got engaged may strike them with the fear. "Oh gosh, do I need to grow up too?!" which of course is entirely unfounded. Your interests and social life may change after marriage, but don't let them sense that they are losing you. You may not want to stay out at the bar until 4am or go on girls-only vacations, but you can enjoy other activities with them that appeal to you both.

Ideas: *Your relationships may change but just continue to make time for them and stay in touch!! Show friends who are acting distantly from you that you still have time for them. Make them feel valued, as they should be to you.*

One Newly Wed's Experience

"When I got engaged, I had mixed reactions from the ladies in my life. Some friends were genuinely excited for me, some perhaps anxious that they were losing me to an institution that they were not yet comfortable with getting close to. The truth is 'marriage' has a stigma with certain people, and this is all too true in the big city. At the time I was living in the city where people around me seemed to be 'Marriage-adverse.'

I said yes to my fiancé because I wanted to be with him forever, and because our ideas regarding career, health, hobbies and overall lifestyle seemed to fit. After we got married, we continued to socialize with friends, see live music, visit comedy clubs, bar hop as well as traveling and hiking...much like we always had. I certainly didn't revert to a life of laundry and aprons like some people had feared I might, and I didn't ditch my best friends.

Things may or may not change—be aware of that and make an extra effort with those friends that fear losing you. Show that that you still have time for them and they'll come to see that things don't have to change like they imagined. This is the 21st century after all."

RSVP Disappointments

There are always going to be some 'no' RSVP's, and some will be more disappointing than others. Perhaps you have an uneven guestlist, (bride or groom-heavy), or you received a no RSVP from someone who you really wished could be there, or were certain would be there. There are always going to be people who can't make it for personal or financial reasons, and it is important that you don't take it personally or feel rejected.

Uneven Guestlists? Perhaps you are getting married in one of your hometowns/ countries, and the other person is receiving a lot of negative RSVP's due to logistical reasons. This can lead to feelings of guilt regarding the location choice, but the reality is that if you are from different places, one person is always going to have more guests than the other.

What you can do: Don't regret your location choice, you obviously made it for a good reason! Have you considered organizing a celebration with the other guests in a second location? This can be within a year of you getting married (before or after the wedding) and still be a special celebration.

One of you is more social/ has a larger family? Since opposites attract, it is fairly common for one person to have a larger social circle or a bigger family than the other. In this case it is only natural that the guestlist is uneven.

What you can do: Again, try not to feel guilty or sad about this. It is unlikely that anyone will notice. His friends and family will become yours after the wedding, and yours will become his, so look forward to that!

Guests you expected to RSVP 'yes' are replying 'no'? You may be given a reason or not, and it is not polite etiquette to ask. Just know that people have their own commitments, it is common (particularly with summer weddings) to have two engagements on the same day, or a whole host of other legitimate reasons. Keep this in mind and remember a time when you had to RSVP 'no' even though you really wished you could make it.

You are not receiving your RSVP's on time - Even though it is basic etiquette, many people forget - or neglect - to RSVP. We all know that an RSVP is important even if it is a no! However, some people don't realize the importance of RSVP-ing until they themselves plan a large event such as a wedding. I am pretty certain that anyone who plans a wedding will never forget to RSVP to another one ever again!

What you can do: Follow up with those stragglers, and give them the benefit of the doubt. A simple phone call or email should help you collect the final responses without wasting your time and energy complaining about it. Some people wait until the last minute to reply, but by explaining politely that you need to give your vendors a final headcount, you should be able to gather together the last of the RSVP's.

On the day you are going to be so happy about those people that can make it, that you will hardly notice those that can't. Trust me!

More than Stress—The Pre-Wedding Blues

"CHANGE IS THE ESSENCE OF LIFE. BE WILLING TO SURRENDER WHAT YOU ARE FOR WHAT YOU COULD BECOME."

- AUTHOR UNKNOWN

Sometimes you might find yourself overwhelmed by anxiety of a different kind. Not the kind of stress you feel when planning an event, moving to a new house or are under a deadline at work. This anxiety is underlined with an uncertainty that creeps up on you unexpectedly. More than just stress, it is closer to **di**stress. And it is the kind that you may be very reluctant to talk about or discuss, even with your best friend or sibling.

You can't quite understand this anxiety and confusion. You are supposed to be in the happiest period of your life, right? Everyone around you discusses the wedding so excitedly and your family, friends, and fiancé are all so thrilled. And so are you, some of the time. At other moments, you just want to run away from it all and throw that goddamn rock off your finger.

He is the man you want to marry, and you are sure of that. But still, on occasion, you doubt the decision to get married at all. This is not how it is supposed to feel when you are going to make vows to be connected with this person for the rest of your life, surely?!

In many situations, feelings of euphoria and excitement are coupled with doubt and confusion, especially under exhaustion.

Nearly every bride feels these pre-wedding blues, yet it remains a fairly taboo topic. While it is seldom talked about, it is important to know that these blues exist and are almost a natural part of the engagement process. All change is scary and overwhelming, even good change. Giving up your single life and talking on a new role, responsibilities, and expectations are no different. Let alone agreeing to take on a new name! This can cause all kinds of identity issues.

This is a major turning point in your life. You have every right to feel fear and sadness, just as you probably did and will in other turning points you reach. Do you remember when you hit puberty and turned into a "young woman?" How about when you left school or home for the first time? The fear of not knowing what is in store for our future leaves us with this anxiety. You are changing from a single woman into a wife, and with this comes more responsibility and possible expectations from society.

It might also mean a change in your relationships with your mother, father, siblings and friends. We hear the expression "my other half," and being in a marriage may feel exactly like that sometimes. You will always have another person, voice, and opinion to consider and may feel like you are losing the freedom being single allowed you to have. But with all of these changes come a lot of positive ones. It is important to focus on these too.

How to Overcome these Pre-Wedding Blues

Modern Matrimony

The truth is, the definition of marriage is changing. We are lucky to live in a world where there are no such rules like there once were. Of course, as a wife there may be certain expectations of you, but no longer are these written in stone In modern relationships we write our own rules to do whatever we can to make them work. You can make it what you always dreamed it would be.

❋ You must be comfortable about the marriage you are entering and ensure that both of you have a good understanding of how you expect it to function. If it is the idea of marriage, and not your partner, that is giving you fear, know that this is somewhat natural and not unexpected. (If, however, it is your partner that you feel uncertain about…that's a whole different conversation.)

❋ Learn to express your emotions. Not everybody will understand, but some will. Try talking to your mother, a recently married friend, or a relative. Explain how you feel. Think about your new role as a wife, and try to get comfortable with the idea. It might take some time, but don't fret. Pre-wedding anxiety is nothing to be overly concerned about. The term "cold-feet" is associated with marriage and weddings for a reason.

❋ External preparations for the wedding day and the short period after it are often the focus for an engaged couple; however, sometimes internal preparations for the marriage need to be made. Addressing the nerves, emotions and fears that accompany your excitement of getting married is really key—try to recognize any issues that might require professional help. This new period of your life is an excellent time to confront existing issues. You have the support of your best friend for life.

Just to reassure you that you are not alone, visit the forums listed in the back of the book and search for the issues I have touched briefly upon in this section. There are thousands of girls before you, and right now, going through the same feelings and emotions. Talk your heart out and work out the best way to deal with them that you can.

"LOVE IS LIKE AN EARTHQUAKE—
UNPREDICTABLE, A LITTLE SCARY, BUT WHEN THE HARD
PART IS OVER YOU REALIZE HOW LUCKY YOU TRULY ARE."

-AUTHOR UNKNOWN

Marriage Rocks

In My Interviews, Newly Weds Told Me Why...

"Cooking proper meals because they are not just for one anymore."

"Constant support whether I am feeling up or really really down."

"Sharing life's responsibilities and errands like decorating and doing the groceries!"

"Receiving hugs on demand." "No more dating drama!"

"Knowing that someone is waiting for you after a night out with the girls."

"Having someone to eat with every night and share the day with."

"Having someone to tell you when you are right..and more importantly when you are wrong. Having someone who knows you inside out."

"Living with your best friend" "Strength, Comfort, Sex!"

"Waking up to fresh coffee every morning."

"Not having to plan my social life in advance—I always have someone to spend the weekend with."

"The benefits and comfort of a double income."

"Having someone to drive when I don't feel like it."

"Having someone to talk to first thing in the morning and last thing at night."

"Being able to argue without worrying too much about the repercussions."

"Having someone who needs and wants me."

"Not feeling insecure about exes or other girls...he's all mine!"

"Always having a plus-one for weddings & parties."

What are you looking forward to?

195

Final Preparations!

24 Hours to Go!

The Day Before

Only 24 hours to go until the day you've been waiting for! Try to relax as much as possible today. It will set you up for a wonderful day tomorrow. You will have last minute things to prepare, guests to welcome and perhaps a rehearsal, but try to keep stress down to a minimum by asking others to help with the chores and getting as much done as possible beforehand so you can enjoy your day.

Morning

1. Wake up and shower—exfoliate/ polish skin well today—especially your arms and chest. Moisturize extra well!

2. Wash your hair if necessary. Whether or not you wash your hair today (or yesterday) will depend on your hair type and the style that you have chosen. Some up-do's require a little grease in order to stay put, as might curly hair. Your natural oils will help your style hold for longer. Consult with your stylist during your trial.

3. Prepare your bag for tomorrow—see the next section: "What to Carry On Your Day."

Afternoon

1. Have a manicure/pedicure scheduled for today.

2. Practice walking in your wedding shoes and break them in if you have not done so already. You love them and you want them to love you back!

Evening

1. Attend your rehearsal (if you are having one)

2. Avoid drinking too much alcohol! Alcohol will disrupt the quality of your sleep. Also limit the amount of caffeine you have today. Avoid salt where possible too—choose a healthy dish or restaurant if you are having a rehearsal dinner. Try to finish eating four hours before bedtime.

3. Get a good night's sleep and have an early night if possible.

What to Carry on Your Day Checklist

(Or: "What Your Best Friend or Bridesmaid Should Carry On Your Day!")

* Sunscreen—opt for a non greasy one. Try *Dermadoctor-Ain't Misbehavin'* SPF 30. This is essential for a summer wedding, or even a spring/autumn one if you will be spending any amount of time outdoors.

* Parasol—for protection against the sun (or rain!) It also doubles as a great prop for pictures.

* Wedding fragrance—this could be your regular favorite scent, or a new one that you can smell for years to come to remind you of your day. (Note: in a hot climate or during the summer avoid wearing too much as scents can be mosquito-attracting.)

* Mosquito spray—particularly if the wedding is near a lake or water.

* Lipstick/gloss

* Bobby pins/hairspray

* Cell phone in order to contact all vendors

* Names and contact info of all vendors

* List of photos that you want taken

* Nail polish—for touch ups. (Do not try to apply while in the car on the way to the venue!)

* Extra tights if you plan to wear them

* Safety pins (small and large)

* Scissors

* Sanitary pads/tampons if necessary

* Mouthwash/breath mints/tooth floss

* Deodorant

* A pair of extra contact lenses if necessary

* Body Spray

* Aspirin

* Double-sided tape

* Tissues

* A nail file

* Q tips—great for taking off smudged makeup from around the eye, or build- up in the corner of the eyes, without making a mess.

* Blotting paper if you are worried about a shiny face. When using this, press—don't rub—to remove grease.

* Compact mirror

* Eye drops

* A sewing kit with needles and thread

* Band aids

* Snacks

The Day Of!

AM

* Eat a combination of carbohydrate and protein, such as scrambled egg on toast, cereal and yogurt, or cream cheese on a whole-wheat bagel. This will keep your energy and stamina levels high throughout the day.

* Take a short walk to boost circulation and reduce any puffiness in your face.

* Use cucumbers/tea bags to reduce any puffiness in your eyes.

* Laugh! Relax. Put on a fun movie or music while you get ready.

Getting Ready

As a rough guide, aim to start getting ready 2-3 hours before the ceremony. (If you are planning to have pre-ceremony/first-look photos, this will need to be earlier. Additionally factor in your transport time). You want adequate time to relax, but not too much time to start getting nervous and playing with your hair, and so on.

Finalize all makeup (except for lipstick) before getting into your dress. Make sure to wear a shirt with buttons so that you do not have to lift it up and over your perfect hair and makeup!

Use the bathroom one last time before getting into your dress.

Drink only water once you are in your dress—avoid colored liquid at all costs.

Now, look at yourself in the mirror, capture this moment in your mind, and take a deep breath.

Enjoy this wonderful day ahead, and have fun!

On the Day—Mishaps, Mayhem & More

"To be prepared is half the victory."

- Miguel De Cervantes

Before I start to worry you, these are worst case scenarios! You already know in the back of your mind that there are going to be butterflies and love and fireworks on your wedding day. It is going to be magical. I could write a whole other book about how wonderful my day was even though I did a lot of worrying before the day itself. That's not to say that things can't go wrong—they can and they will!

I'll share a secret with you—10 days before my wedding I found out that I couldn't take my wedding dress on the plane back to England with me. It was a horrible miscommunication between myself, the wedding shop, and the airline, but I realized that I had to do something about the situation fast. I cried and then I did what everyone else would do in that situation. I found a solution without fretting too much. The things that go "wrong" are outside of your control, and the only thing that you can control is your reaction.

So, start the day with a sense of humor and know that no matter what happens, everything always works out in the end! (I wore a different dress, purchased the day before I left the country and one that would fit in my hand luggage, and sold the other one online. I loved the second dress just as much!)

1. Rain

According to Hindu tradition, rain on your wedding day is actually considered good luck!

Rainy photos can look super romantic. Consider using props such as umbrellas, rain boots and pose in cozy out-of-the-way spots. Just be sure to have a Plan B in the event of rain, and stay in high spirits. Turn lemons into lemonade—rain will create an atmosphere of warmth and intimacy, plus give unfamiliar guests an extra thing to talk about!

Tips:

- Wear waterproof everything—foundation, mascara eye shadow

- Be sure to have hairspray and pins at hand for frizz control.

- Be prepared with umbrellas...

- Enjoy the feelings of warmth that the rain can bring

2. Zits

When I surveyed Brides-to-Be about their biggest fears regarding the big day, would you be surprised to hear that, a BIG RED ZIT was on the top of nearly every Bride-to-Be's list?

If this happens to you (or even if you feel one coming on the day before) try:

* Using a treatment with salicylic acid (2%) and sulfur on the point in question. These are both anti-inflammatory agents that shrink and calm pimples by penetrating the follicle, exfoliate, and clear out the pore all in one. Be careful not to apply it to areas that don't need it as it will dry the skin out.

* Wear a good concealer! Look for a corrective one with a green undertone, which counteracts the redness of pimples.

* Avoid touching it at all costs. Really!

3. Being on Your Period on Your Day

The thought of being on your period might not faze you or it might be driving you stir-crazy. It all depends on how much grief your little friend gives you each month, both the week before and during the week itself.

Many women opt to use the contraceptive pill to control when their period will arrive. If you are not already taking the pill, this might be an option; however, keep in mind that by its very nature (hormones), the pill may cause side-effects and it is not unusual to try two or three different kinds before finding one that vibes well with your own body. Trying the pill so soon before the wedding is a risky endeavor particularly bearing in mind the potential side effects of weight gain, change in breast size and skin changes.

Dealing With Menstrual Cramps (Also see PMS section)

* **Medicine**: Your regular painkiller. Always read the label, and only take if you have taken them before to avoid unwanted side effects. Taking painkillers when you start to feel the symptoms rather than waiting for the cramps to become more pronounced is the most effective way to deal with them.

* **Try Heat Packs**: Heat can do wonders for cramping and pain. ThermaCare (thermacare.com) offers a Lower Back and Hip heat wrap that will provide some relief from cramps. Otherwise microwaveable heat pads can be found in most drugstores. Doing this the morning before the wedding should help a lot throughout the day.

* **Drink Warm Drinks**: Herbal and chamomile tea, or anything without caffeine.

* **Exercise**: You may not feel like it but light and gentle exercise—stretching, a walk, dancing and so on—will prevent your muscles from becoming tense and tight.

* **Consume Calcium**: Adequate calcium intake is thought to minimize menstrual discomfort. Bananas are high in calcium and magnesium, which is also thought to be helpful at this time of the month. Of course there are many dairy foods that are high in calcium, but it is thought that dairy products may worsen your symptoms.

* **Drink Plenty of Water**

* **Eat Foods Rich in Fiber:** Fiber is particularly useful in cleansing the body of excess estrogen, which may contribute to menstrual cramps.

Peeing In Your Dress

Don't freak out if you haven't already thought about this. It's a tricky situation but a road many ladies before you have traveled on. With a little strategy, I thoroughly believe this is going to be one of your favorite wedding memories…and also your Mom, Sis or BFF's!

First of all, scope out the bathroom situation. Check if the floor is clean. Is there a disabled bathroom? If so, you are in luck! Extra space is good.

How the situation is going to pan out will depend not only on the bathroom available, but also on the type of dress you are wearing. You should alter the method depending upon what your circumstances are, but here are some general pointers to keep you on the right track!

Step 1: You might want to take off your underwear completely rather than just letting them sit around your ankles.

Step 2: Face the toilet and pull the dress up around your waist. Depending on the bulkiness of your dress, this is where you might want to enlist the help of a BM or family member.

Step 3: Straddle the toilet still facing it, i.e. backwards to how you would usually pee. Sounds odd, but there will be a lot more space for your dress behind you rather than in front of you. There will be no chance for you to get it wet or dirty by doing it this way.

Step 4: Laugh hysterically!

Voilà ma chérie :)

Shutterbugging Secrets
How to look GREAT in your pictures!

"**FOR BEAUTIFUL EYES, LOOK FOR THE GOOD IN OTHERS; FOR BEAUTIFUL LIPS, SPEAK ONLY WORDS OF KINDNESS; AND FOR POISE, WALK WITH THE KNOWLEDGE THAT YOU ARE NEVER ALONE.**"

-**AUDREY HEPBURN**

The Art of Posing, Choosing Flattering Light and a Natural Smile

There are a few tips and tricks stolen from supermodels, life models, and Hollywood actresses that you might want to know in order to look your best in the wedding pictures. They don't take much effort to remember and will drastically improve your shots so you can feel confident about being in front of the camera.

About the Pose

"**DARLING, THE LEGS AREN'T SO BEAUTIFUL, I JUST KNOW WHAT TO DO WITH THEM.**"

-**MARLENE DIETRICH**

The camera can add ten pounds—or shake ten pounds if you are standing the right way and deceiving it. Focus on the posture you always knew you should have—shoulders back, chin up and breasts forward (but obviously not too aggressively). This will elongate the torso, flatter the arms and shoulders, and avoid any double chin shots.

If you stand head-on to the camera, your hips will appear wide and bulky. Try turning to the side and then angling one shoulder back to face the camera. This is particularly easy to do if you are in the shot with hubby—you can stand towards him and then face the camera.

If you are hoping to look a little slimmer, keep your elbows away from the body. That distance between your torso and arms will give a slimmer outline, whereas if your arms are in front of the body, pounds will be added to the visual. When holding your bouquet, hold it low and with straight arms, this will be very flattering on your waist and hips.

Camera Angle

This is really the photographer's expertise, but if you are taking your own pics before you leave the house or at any other time, ask the photographer to shoot from a high angle rather than a low one. This way the eyes and face are closer to the camera and the body appears smaller. It is so much more flattering than a shot from below or even from at eye level.

Lighting

Avoid taking pictures in direct sunlight as this will lead to squinting and a pale, unfavorable complexion. Although we can't control the weather, an overcast day lends itself to lovely lighting, as does the early morning and just before sunset.

Smile

Your smile should look natural—smile with the eyes, not just your mouth! It is SO obvious when someone is not genuinely smiling! But, you might not feel like flashing an authentic smile for the entire duration of the photo session, so how do avoid that fake smile?

Well, first of all, try to make your hubby* laugh, and encourage him to do the same. You can tell each other silly jokes, recall stupid happenings from the past or just try your best to enjoy yourself. One of my favorite tips is to take a deep breath in, and then as you breathe out, a natural attractive smile will follow. Splendid!

(*Yes, he is no longer referred to as hubby-to-be!)

Practice posing and smiling for the camera confidently! Know which angles you look best from and take note of simple changes such as placing your arm in such a manner that looks flattering.

Jet Lag

Jet lag is a funny thing—who knew that our bodies were so intelligent at telling the time? No matter how hard we try to get acquainted with the new time zone, jet lag often hits throughout the day with symptoms that include not being able to fall asleep even though we feel tired, being tired at the wrong times, irritability, stomach problems, and generally not quite feeling "present."

The more time zones you cross, the worse your jet lag will be. Roughly speaking, one time zone will take one day to recover. For example, the East Coast US to Europe is 5 zones, so it will take around 5 days to adjust fully. Traveling East (US—Europe) is usually harder to adjust to than traveling West (US—Asia).

Ways to Minimize Jet Lag

Before

* The day before your flight, try to eat light, do some gentle exercise, and avoid salt as much as possible.

* Avoid big meals before taking off as it is harder to digest food when flying (with all of the sitting down)

* Also try to avoid eating foods that produce excess gas as they will expand in your stomach and cause bloating. This includes (but is not limited to) onions, cauliflower, broccoli, cabbage, and beans.

During

* **Drink Plenty of Water**—The humidity in many airliners is very low (2-3%). This makes you very dehydrated and will contribute to feeling lousy at your destination. Try to drink a glass of water every hour and choose it over soda or alcohol.

* **Get Up and Stretch Frequently**—It's not natural to be sat down for long periods of time anyway, but especially not at high altitudes. Getting up and about will keep your blood circulating and will benefit your digestive system, too.

* **Avoid Alcohol**—Skip in-flight drinks as lower oxygen levels and the increase in pressure will mean the effects of alcohol are felt much more strongly. (It may be the cheapest way you ever got drunk!)

* **Loosen Your Shoes.**

After

* When you arrive, resist the urge to sleep until nighttime. This means no napping! Doing so will help you get into a routine for the rest of the trip. Change your watch to avoid thinking about what time it is 'back home' and try to get acquainted with the new time as soon as possible.

Bonus Section: Grooming the Grooms

Let's be honest—when it comes to beauty, guys have it easy. Hubby-to-be is probably not interested in stepping up his grooming routine too much, and there is no need for him to go OTT. Males are pretty damn attractive without much effort. But this is the 21st century and no longer is it shameful for him to be a little bit metro-sexual and hold some form of skincare routine. In fact, it's sexy and I like it!

There are a few things he might want to pay attention to since he will also be the center of attention and will want to look his best.

Skin

Often guys have larger pores than us gals, and this is the reason why they can have larger, more predominant (and stubborn) blackheads. Particularly if they have sat there undisturbed since middle school, it may be hard to shake them off. If this is the case, encourage him to visit the salon for a facial at least once before the wedding.

Avoiding the Salon—His At-home Facial

If your guy doesn't want to visit a professional for an extraction (though it is recommended), there are some at-home facial methods you can suggest to him. If blackheads are the problem, encourage him to use the steam bath method to open up his pores. See page 32 for instructions.

Exfoliation

Encourage him to use an exfoliator 2-3 times a week to keep blackheads at bay, and using a moisturizer will help keep his pores small and closed. Even oily skin can be dehydrated—remember that oil and moisture are two different things.

Hair

Hair should be cut one-two weeks before the day to look smart but natural. Mousse, wax or gel can keep hair in place on a windy day.

Excess Hair

Eyebrows and nose hair can easily be taken care of and many hair salons will offer this service on request during a haircut.

Teeth Whitening

Encourage him to join your whitening routine. See page 13.

MANicures

Hands will also be on show for the ring pictures and cake cutting. Clean nails are a must!

Water

Guys generally need 10-12 glasses a day. Cutting back on caffeine and alcohol will also improve his complexion and energy levels.

Chapped Lips

You do have to kiss him at the altar after all! Lip balm works wonders.

His List of Must-Haves on The Day

* Shoes are buffed and shined. Labels on the underside of the shoes have been removed.

* Deodorant.

* Necessary hairstyling products.

* Moisturizer.

* Toothbrush, toothpaste, floss and mouthwash.

* Sunscreen if necessary.

* Lip balm.

* Your favorite cologne!

* Make sure that his suit & shirt are wrinkle-free and labels have been removed.

The Final Word

And so we have come to the end! I hope you are revved up and excited for that day you have waited a long time for. It's going to be a blast. Don't forget to enjoy it! Sneak a few minutes here and there with each other to reflect on what is going on around you. Someone suggested this to me and it was great advice - the feeling is surreal.

I've said it before but it's worth saying again. Understandably, you want to look and feel your best for your big day. But you should really aim to "glow" on both your day AND in your marriage, which is the weeks, months, and years that follow the wedding day itself. I hope this book has among other things peaked your interest in keeping your body and mind in shape for life. Sometimes your physical and mental health need working on, so don't forget to give them the attention they deserve.

That way you can enjoy life and all that it brings you to the absolute fullest!

Don't forget to find me on:

Facebook - glowing.bride

Twitter - glowingbride

& at www.wowglowingbride.com.

I love hearing from readers and I'm here to answer your pre-wedding related questions so leave a comment, ask questions or tweet me!

Stay Glowing and Congratulations!

Laura

Further Resources

Appendix A: Popular Wedding Forums & Websites to Gain Support

Project Wedding - http://www.projectwedding.com/topic/list

WeddingBee Boards http://boards.weddingbee.com/

Wedding Wire Forums - http://www.weddingwire.com/wedding-forums/

Bridal Tweet - http://www.bridaltweet.com/forum

OneWed - http://forums.onewed.com/index.php

Offbeat Bride Tribe - http://offbeatbride.ning.com/

Brides.com - http://www.brides.com/forums/index.jspa

Wedding Channel - http://forums.weddingchannel.com/Main.aspx

Bridal Guide - http://www.bridalguide.com/community/messageboards/

The Knot Forums - http://wedding.theknot.com/wedding-message-boards

Appendix B: Books & Websites

Here are some books I recommend for further reading on topics that I have touched upon, but were beyond the scope of this book:

Section 1: Beauty

Saeki, Chizu, *The Japanese Skincare Revolution: How to Have the Most Beautiful Skin of Your Life--At Any Age*. Kodansha International, 2009.

Consumer Reports on Whitening Products: **http://www.consumerreports.org/** "and search tooth whiteners August 2009"

YouTube Makeup Videos:

1. Makeup By Tiffany D **www.youtube.com/user/MakeupByTiffanyD**

2. Panacea81 (Lauren Luke) **www.youtube.com/user/panacea81**.

3. MakeupGeekTV **http://www.youtube.com/user/MakeupGeekTV**

Section 2: Health

Kimiko Barber, *The Chopsticks Diet: Japanese-inspired Recipes for Easy Weight-Loss*. Kyle Books, 2009.

Heather Van Vorous & David B. Posner, *The First Year: IB—An Essential Guide for the Newly Diagnosed*. Da Capo Press, 2005.

Mark Pimentel, *A New IBS Solution*. Health Point Press, 2005.

Carolyn Dean MD ND & L. Christine Wheeler MA, *IBS Cookbook for Dummies, For Dummies, 2009.*

Heather Van Vorous, *Eating for IBS: 175 Delicious, Nutritious, Low-Fat, Low-Residue Recipes to Stabilize the Touchiest Tummy*. Da Capo Press, 2000.

Eat This, Not That series:

David Zinczenko & Matt Goulding, *Eat This Not That! 2010: The No-Diet Weight Loss Solution*, Rodale Books, 2009.

David Zinczenko & Matt Goulding, *Eat This Not That! Supermarket Survival Guide*, Rodale Books, 2008

David Zinczenko & Matt Goulding, *Eat This Not That! Restaurant Survival Guide*, Rodale Books, 2009

David Zinczenko & Matt Goulding, *Cook This Not That! Kitchen Survival Guide*, Rodale Books, 2009

Useful Nutrition Websites

RDA website - http://fnic.nal.usda.gov

www.healthydiningfinder.com

http://www.starbucks.com/

http://www.caloriecounter.com/

www.whfoods.com/fdanalyzer.php

PMDD website - http://www.pmddinformation.com/

Section 3: Well-Being

Adrian Williams, *Insomnia: Doctor I Can't Sleep*, Amberwood Publishing Ltd,1996.

Harvard Medical School. Division of Sleep Medicine. www.hms.harvard.edu/sleep.

http://www.stressfulworld.com

National Sleep Foundation - http://www.sleepfoundation.org.

Other

Yelp – www.yelp.com

A great resource to find salons, spas and services in your area

http://www.allure.com/directory - Spa and salon directory.

Appendix C: Deals

Here are a few of the online organizations that provide health, beauty, lifestyle, and restaurant coupons, at a discount of 50% and more. Just sign up for daily deals in your area and life is suddenly more affordable! (Note: some are in limited locations/major cities only.)

Daily candy - http://www.dailycandy.com/all-cities/deals/ - numerous cities.

Lifebooker - http://nyc.lifebooker.com/welcome

Groupon - www.groupon.com - several cities.

Living Social - http://livingsocial.com/

Appendix D: Super Foods Shopping List

As you found out on page 107, super foods are nutrient-dense foods that are great for a number of reasons, both in terms of health and well-being. Here is an easy reference for you -try to include at least five super foods on your shopping list each week and mix it up each week.

1. **Berries**—strawberries, blueberries, blackberries, etc.

2. **Nuts**—unsalted, unroasted. Walnuts are a particularly nutritious option.

3. **Whole grains**—brown bread, brown rice, cereals, cereal bars. Look for the "Whole Grains" logo.

4. **Dark greens**—broccoli, asparagus, kale, chard, collard, green beans, bok choy.

5. **Flax seeds**

6. **Oily fish**—especially salmon.

7. **Tea**—Green tea or white tea.

8. **Chocolate** – Dark, organic.

9. **Yogurt**—Plain, low fat, not low sugar or light versions. Or a probiotic like Yakult.

10. **Tomato**

11. **Eggs**

12. **Bananas**

Other—Red wine, beans, dried fruit (no preservatives), sweet potatoes.

Supplements (if necessary): Vitamin C, Fish or Flaxseed oil, Coenzyme Q10.

Acknowledgements/Thank Yous

To those who helped shape the book, and endured me in the process, big love! Clare Bradwell, Rebecca Minton, Caroline Pepper, Karen Pepper, Connie Lo, Brandy Gamoning, Suzanne Ogden Vannatter, Rhian Davies, Isabella Li and Eva Liao.

I also wish to thank the hundreds of brides who helped answer my questions and surveys. Without you, this book would still be an idea floating around my mind.

Christine Marie Bryant and the wonderful members of the Coffee House Writers Group. An endless source of inspiration, motivation and fun times, I am so happy to have you in my life!

And Brandon... your input in the book is greater than you will ever realize. I love you dearly.

My superb bridesmaids, obviously. You were amazing!

My A-List

(Please contact me for contact information)

Model: Leah Grounds

Editor: Allison Itterly

Designer: Catalin Slutu

Index